An Overview Series Publication

Computer Architectures

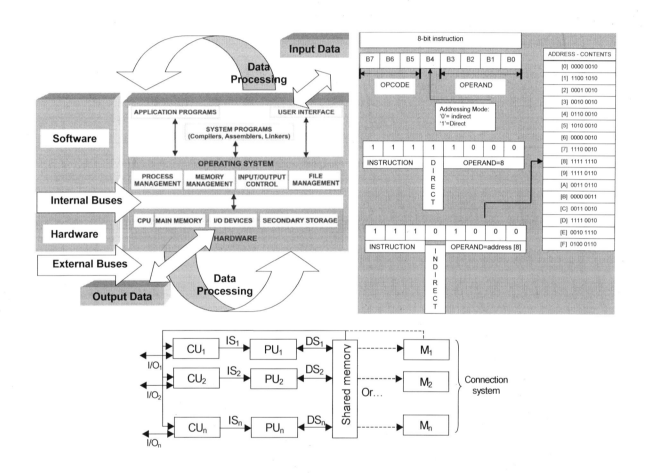

Dr. Goran I Bezanov PhD

This page is intentionally left blank

COMPUTER ARCHITECTURES

AN OVERVIEW SERIES PUBLICATION

By Goran Bezanov PhD

MIG Consulting Ltd

31 Vicarage Road, London SW14 8RZ

British Library Cataloguing in Publication Data

A catalogue record for this book is available from the British Library

International Standard Book Number: 978-0-9558153-4-8

To my Sons

Ognen and Milos

This page is intentionally left blank

PREFACE

This text is a very brief overview of computer architectures. My aim was to write a text that can be read and understood by readers who are not overly familiar with modern computer systems. It was my intention that, from this text they could gain sufficient understanding in order to know where to look for further direction. In Chapters 1-4 I cover briefly topics relating to general computer hardware architecture and the role of the operating system. Here I deal with areas such as process management and memory management in order to give the reader an idea of the type of workload a computer on a typical network, may need to cope with.

Chapter 5 deals with issues relating to CPU design. General features of an 8-bit CPU are considered and a typical instruction set is designed. There follows an example of a simulator written in C programming language. This is done to illustrate how the instructions are processed inside the Control Unit.

Chapters 6 and 7 introduce the more advanced architecture topics such as pipelining and scaling. In particular Chapter 7 deals with parallel processing including the programming aspects for parallel execution.

This is my first draft and I shall revise and correct the errors in the next. Suggestions welcome to: mig@consultant.com.

Thank you

Goran Bezanov (December 2009, London)

This page is intentionally left blank

CONTENTS

CHAPTER 1 COMPUTER ARCHITECTURE

1.1. Introduction

In computer systems, architecture refers to the conceptual design and fundamental operational structure of a computer system. In a general sense however computer architecture focuses on the way in which the central processing unit (CPU) performs in order to facilitate accurate and efficient operation of the computer system.

That said, computer systems comprise a complex combination of software and hardware components and therefore it is not uncommon to consider the hardware and the software architectures of a computer system separately even thought they combine to provide a complete solution to the design of a computer system. Thus on the one hand computer architecture can be used to describe the process of selecting and interconnecting hardware components to create computers that meet functional, performance and cost goals. And on the other hand, looking at the software, it can describe the blueprint for the requirements and design implementations for the various parts of a computer system. In a general sense however computer architecture comprises at least three main subcategories, namely Industry standard architecture, microarchitecture and system architecture. [1]

Instruction set architecture (ISA): This is an abstract representation of a computer system that is seen by a machine language (or assembly language) programmer. This includes the instruction set, memory address modes, processor registers, and address and data formats. In other words, if the computer system is to perform some useful processing, the instructions that it supports constitute a set, which define its architecture at this level. At this level, the architecture would describe the number of registers used for data, address, and the stack as well as the flags register, all of which combine to provide the functionality of the computer system from a programming viewpoint.

1

Microarchitecture: This refers to the level below the instruction set architecture providing a more detailed description of the system. For example, when an instruction set has been defined, and a program written that supports this set, the microarchitecture describes the processing of these instructions. This includes a description of how the constituent parts of the system are interconnected and how they interoperate in order to implement the ISA. For example, the microarchitecture would typically describe the way that the internal registers are organised and how the instructions are decoded in the control unit.

System architecture: This is perhaps the most intuitive of the three and it describes how the hardware components within a computing system are interconnected. For example it would describe:

1.   How internal components of the computer system interconnect with each other. (i.e. computer buses, peripherals etc)

2.   How memory is organised and how memory controllers are used to bridge between the various storage devices in the memory hierarchy. For example, I/O access is much slower that access to a level 2 CACHE memory. In order for the system to function optimally buses of different speeds are provided and bridges between these are used to enable synchronisation.

3.   How supporting mechanisms are implemented to relieve the CPU. For example, direct memory access (DMA) controllers are used to bypass the CPU when transferring data between devices.

4.   How issues like multi-processing, parallel processing, clustering etc are implemented. For example, the Windows NT O/S provides the software that facilitates symmetric multi processing (SMP). This means that a number of CPUs can be used at the same time to share the processing workload. For example, when Microsoft programmers developed the O/S they needed to understand the system architecture of the Intel Pentium family of processors in order to provide the system software to support SMP. The same principle applies if the programmers were to develop the SMP capability on other hardware platforms.

1.2. Basic components of computer architecture

A modern computer system consists of a combination of software and hardware components all of which combine to enable the computer system to process data efficiently and accurately. Each of these components in its own right is a complex system itself, which can be subdivided further.

In order to illustrate this Figure 1.1 shows a simplified view of a typical computer system. Here the system is split into the software and the hardware sections.

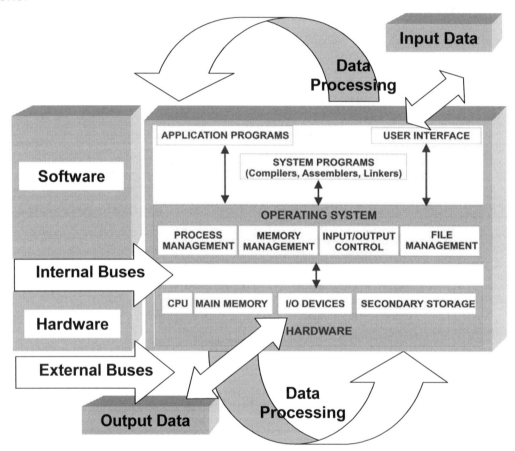

Figure 1.1. Components of a computer system

The hardware includes the central processing unit (CPU) and main memory. This is random access memory (RAM) that is used to store the programme code being executed. The CPU and RAM communicate over internal buses, which are much faster than external buses. The external buses are the Input/Output (I/O) buses that are used to connect I/O devices such as video displays, hard disks, network interface cards (NICs) etc.

In a very broad sense buses can be thought of as a number of parallel conductors that connect components. The number of these parallel lines determines the width of a bus. For example, 32-bit bus will have 32 parallel conductors connecting each device that needs to use the bus. The devices that are connected to it determine the actual speed of the bus. Peripheral devices such as hard disks are much slower than for example RAM access, and therefore there is no point trying to connect the hard disk to the CPU using a high-speed bus. More details will be given later in Chapter 4 of this text. Figure 1.1 also shows that the computer system software is made up of a number of components. The top part of Figure 1.1 is the user software and this includes the application programs, the user interface, and software programming and development tools. Below this is the operating system (O/S) software, which is a set of programs that enable access to the internal computer hardware. In a general sense the O/S performs tasks, such as for example, recognising keyboard input, displaying output to screen, keeping track of files and directories on the disk and controlling peripheral devices such as disk drives, printers, network interfaces, modems etc. It is also responsible for security, preventing unauthorised user access to the system. The block diagram of Figure 1.2 illustrates some operations that an operating system is concerned with. Here to distinguish between internal and external operations, the components shaded in grey are I/O oriented.

Most general purpose O/Ss support multitasking, which means that a number of different programs can run at the same time, i.e. concurrently. As seen in Figure 1.2, one of the jobs of the O/S is process management. The O/S performs overall monitoring of tasks ensuring that different programs, which are running concurrently do not interfere with each other. Since all tasks that are running have to be loaded into physical RAM, during process control the O/S needs to consider the activity of the CPU and also to look after memory management.

Another function of the O/S is to provide a platform on top of which application programs can run. Typical examples of software applications are word processors, spreadsheets, media players etc. Management of peripheral devices such as the display, keyboard, printer etc. is another key role of the O/S.

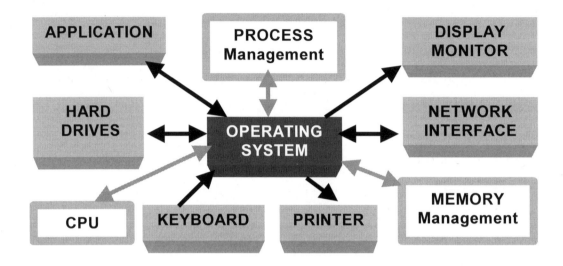

Figure 1.2. Operating system interfacing to programs and peripherals

1.3. Types of operating systems

O/Ss are developed by programmers in order to provide users of the computer system with a capability to run programs for their specific needs. A general purpose O/S such as Windows or Linux is designed with a different aim from; say a real-time O/S. In the early 1980's the DOS operating system was perhaps the most common type of system used with the original IBM compatible PC range. It was a general purpose O/S, which although limited by modern standards, enabled programmers to develop some very useful computer applications. There are many different types of operating systems but some characteristic types are as follows,

- **Multi-user**- allows two or more users to run programs at the same time. Some operating systems permit hundreds or even thousands of concurrent users.

- **Multiprocessing**- Supports the running of programs on more than one CPU, such as SMP mentioned earlier.

- **Multitasking**- allows more than one program to run concurrently (i.e. at the same time).

- **Multithreading**- allows different parts of a single program to run concurrently.
- **Real time-** Responds to input within a specific time, which is determined by the so-called real-time constraints.
- **Network**- A network operating system performs the functions of multi-user, multiprocessing and multitasking operating systems and additionally, implements protocol stacks as well as device drivers for networking hardware.

In order to illustrate the different uses of O/Ss Table 1.1 shows a brief list of the non real-time O/Ss and their target applications. [2] Table 1.2 depicts some of the real-time O/Ss that are still in use today.

Table 1.1 Comparison of various non-RT O/S systems

Name	Creator	First public release	Latest release date	Target system type
AIX	IBM	1986	2007-11-?	Server, NetApp, Workstation
AmigaOS	Amiga, Inc.	1985	2008-09-16	Workstation, Home Desktop
FreeBSD	The FreeBSD Project	1993	2009-01-05	Server, Workstation, NetApp, Embedded
Haiku	Haiku Inc.	-	(Nightly builds)	Home Desktop
HP-UX	Hewlett-Packard	1983	2007-02-15	Server, Workstation
IBM i	IBM	1988	2008-04-?	Server
IRIX	SGI	1988	2006-08-16	Server, Workstation
Inferno	Bell Labs	1997	2007-02-?	NetApp, Server, Embedded
GNU/Linux	Linus Torvalds, et al.	1992	2008-12-14; 2007-10-23	See: Comparison of Linux distributions
Mac OS	Apple Inc.	1984	2002-05-12	Workstation, home desktop
Mac OS X	Apple Inc.	2001	2008-12-15	Workstation, Home Desktop, Mobile (embedded)
Mac OS X Server	Apple Inc.	2001	2008-12-15	Server
Minix3	Andrew S. Tanenbaum	2005	2006-05-29	Workstation
NetBSD	The NetBSD Project	1993	2008-10-14	NetApp, Server, Workstation, Embedded
NeXTStep	NeXT	1989	1995-02-01	Workstation
NetWare	Novell	1985	2007-10-?	Server
OpenBSD	The OpenBSD Project	1995	2008-11-01	Server, NetApp, Workstation, Embedded
OpenVMS	DEC (now HP)	1977	2007-10-?	Server, Workstation
OS/2	IBM and Microsoft	1987	2001-12-?	Home Desktop, Server
PC-BSD	PC-BSD Software	2006	2008-04-23	Desktop, Workstation, Server

Name	Creator	First public release	Latest release date	Target system type
Plan 9	Bell Labs	1993	(Daily snapshots)	Workstation, Server, Embedded, HPC
QNX	QNX Software Systems	1982	2006-09-28	Workstation, Server, Embedded
Solaris	Sun	1992	2008-04-15	Server, Workstation
Windows Server (NT family)	Microsoft	1993	2008-02-27	Server, NetApp, Embedded, HPC
Microsoft Windows (NT family)	Microsoft	1985	2006 November - 2007 January [8]	Workstation, Home Desktop, media center, Tablet PC, embedded
RISC OS	Acorn Computers, RISC OS Limited, Castle Technology Ltd	1989	2008-05-28	Educational desktop, home computer
ZETA	yellowTAB	2005	2006-04-27	Home Desktop, Media Workstation
STOP 6 / XTS-400	BAE Systems	2003-?-?	2007-06-?	Server, Workstation, cross-domain solution, network guard
ReactOS	ReactOS development team	1996-?-?	2008-08-06	Workstation, Home Desktop
z/OS	IBM	2000	2007	IBM mainframe

Table 1.2 Real time O/S comparisons

Name	Target usage	Platforms
BeRTOS	Embedded	DSP56K, I196, IA32, ARM, AVR
ChibiOS/RT	Embedded, small footprint	x86, ARM7, ARM Cortex-M3, AVR, MSP430
CMX RTOS	Embedded	IA32, ARM, AVR, H8, PIC, 8051
Contiki	Embedded	MSP430, AVR
eCos	General purpose	ARM/XScale, CalmRISC, 68000/Coldfire, fr30, FR-V, H8, IA32, MIPS, MN10300, OpenRISC, PowerPC, SPARC, SuperH, V8xx
eCosPro	General purpose	ARM/XScale, CalmRISC, 68000/Coldfire, fr30, FR-V, H8, IA32, MIPS, MN10300, NIOS2, OpenRISC, PowerPC, SPARC, SuperH, V8xx
embOS	embedded	8/16/32 bit processors
Femto OS	embedded	AVR
FreeRTOS	embedded	ARM, AVR, AVR32, HCS12, IA32, MicroBlaze, MSP430, PIC, Renesas H8/S, 8052
Fusion RTOS	semi-general purpose	ARM, Blackfin, StarCore, DSP 56800E
INTEGRITY	?	ARM, XScale, Blackfin, Freescale ColdFire, MIPS, PowerPC, x86
LynxOS	?	Motorola 68010, Intel 80386, ARM, PowerPC
MERT	?	PDP-11

Name	Target usage	Platforms
MicroC/OS-II	embedded	AVR, ...
Nano-RK	embedded	AVR, MSP430
Neutrino	microkernel	ARM, MIPS, PPC, SH, x86, XScale
Nucleus OS	embedded	AMD Au1100, ARM, Atmel AT91 series, Atmel Nios II, Freescale iMX, Freescale MCF, Freescale MPC, Marvell PXA series, MTI, NEC uPD6111x, Sharp LH7 series, ST, TI OMAP, TI TMS320 series, Xilinx Microblaze
OSE	general purpose	ARM, PowerPC, MIPS, IXP2400, TI OMAP, ...
OS-9	?	ARM/strongARM, MIPS, PowerPC, SuperH, x86/Pentium, XSCALE, Motorola 6809, Motorola 68000-series
OSEK	embedded	engine control units
PICOS18	embedded	PIC18
Prex	microkernel	ARM, IA32
QNX	general purpose	IA32, MIPS, PowerPC, SH-4, ARM, StrongARM, XScale
RMX	?	8080, 8086, 80386 or higher
RTEMS	embedded	ARM, Blackfin, ColdFire, TI C3x/C4x, H8/300, x86, 68k, MIPS, Nios II, PowerPC, SuperH, SPARC, ERC32, LEON, Mongoose-V
RTLinux	general purpose	same as Linux
SimpleAVROS	Embedded	AVR only
Symbian OS	?	ARM
Talon DSP RTOS	embedded DSP	TMS320
ThreadX	?	ARC, ARM/Thumb, AVR32, BlackFin, ColdFire/68K, H8/300H, Luminary Micro Stellaris, M-CORE, MicroBlaze, PIC24/dsPIC, PIC32, MIPS, V8xx, Nios II, PowerPC, SH, SHARC, StarCore, STM32, StrongARM, TMS320C54x, TMS320C6x, x86/x386, XScale, Xtensa/Diamond, ZSP
Trampoline Operating System	embedded	AVR, H8/300H, POSIX, NEC V850e, ARM7, Infineon C166, HCS12 or PowerPC
Transaction Processing Facility	general purpose	IBM System/360 derivatives
TRON Project	mixed	any
velOSity	?	Power Architecture, ARM/XScale, MIPS, x86/Pentium, ColdFire, Blackfin, OMAP, DaVinci
VxWorks	embedded	ARM, IA32, MIPS, PowerPC, SH-4, StrongARM, xScale
Windows CE	?	x86, MIPS, ARM, SuperH

The tables given here serve simply to show the variety of O/S at the time of preparing this textbook. There are also O/Ss that have been designed for specific hardware and therefore they do not have a broad area of application. For example the VAL-II O/S is used in programming robotic mechanisms. As automatic manufacturing systems become more sophisticated, there is an increasing need for advanced robots, which can be easily integrated into the overall system. These robots need to interact with both a supervisory control network and with various sensory devices. VAL-II is a robot control system and programming language, which addresses these needs by supporting network communications, general sensory interfaces, real-time trajectory modification, and concurrent user-program execution. In addition, VAL-II includes high-level computer programming facilities that allow professional programmers to develop special-purpose application programs, which simplify the operator interface. [3]

1.4. Computer software

Computer software offers a degree of flexibility that is not so easily provided by the hardware. By software programming, the hardware can be made to function in different ways. Figure 1.3 provides a simplified view of the computer programming hierarchy. Here the levels of programming are split into a number of categories at different levels of the hierarchy. The hierarchical decomposition is used to show that every level depends on the one below it for operation.

Software programming at high and low level includes system software, application software, program loader, I/O control system etc. The development tools that are used include compilers, linkers, loaders and debugging tools. Application programming usually requires a run-time library to enable portability. Operational and end users typically use scripting tools to write programs. Some visual programming tools include a GUI to simplify the programming task (i.e. Visual Basic). With reference to Figure 1.3 a brief explanation of some software components is given as follows,

User programming

This type of programming refers to general users who have not been formally taught how to program in a conventional high level programming language (i.e. C++, VBasic, Java etc). These languages are designed for users to change the actions and/or user interface of a system. For example, AutoCad has an embedded Lisp language for extensions, and Microsoft Word for Windows has an embedded Visual Basic language. These are user-programming languages that can be used to enhance the application from the user perspective. End user programmers also include, self-taught Webmasters writing JavaScript; network administrators writing logon scripts and script to configure routers; experts in complex business automation tools like SAP (Systems, Applications, Products). [4]

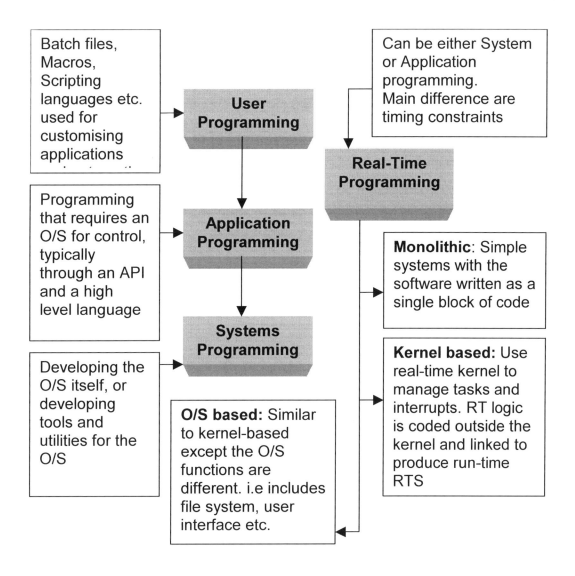

Figure 1.3. Computer programming hierarchy

Application Programming

This type of programming utilises an Application Programming Interface (API) to develop programs that run on the platform for which the API has been developed. [5] In computer program development, APIs are a set of routines, protocols, and tools for building software applications. A good API makes it easier to develop a program by providing all the building blocks, which can be easily put together by a programmer. Most operating environments, such as Windows, provide an API so that programmers can write applications that are consistent with the operating system. Although APIs are designed for programmers, they are also good for users because they guarantee that all programs using a common API will have similar interfaces. This makes it easier for users to learn new programs.

Systems programming

Systems programming produces the software that provides services to the computer hardware. Examples include implementing certain parts of the O/S such as for example the paging system (Virtual Memory) a disk defragmenter or a device driver for a network operating system. This level of programming requires a greater degree of hardware understanding by the programmer. More specifically, the programmer will utilise the properties of the hardware in order to write efficient code to perform systems functions. Originally systems programmers coded programs in assembly language. However, with the growth of the UNIX operating system, C language emerged as a viable and efficient systems programming language. (i.e. UNIX was written in C). An object-oriented variant of C namely C++, was used for O/S development such as the Windows NT and embedded C++ is used to write the I/O Kit drivers of Mac OS X. To illustrate the different levels of programming an example of the Windows 2000 architecture is shown in Figure 1.4. Here it is seen that the architecture is divided into two parts, the User mode and the Kernel mode. User mode refers to all the applications, services, system processes and the environment subsystem, all of which go through the dynamic link library in order to access the kernel mode. The kernel is part of the operating system that provides the very basic services for all other parts of the operating system.

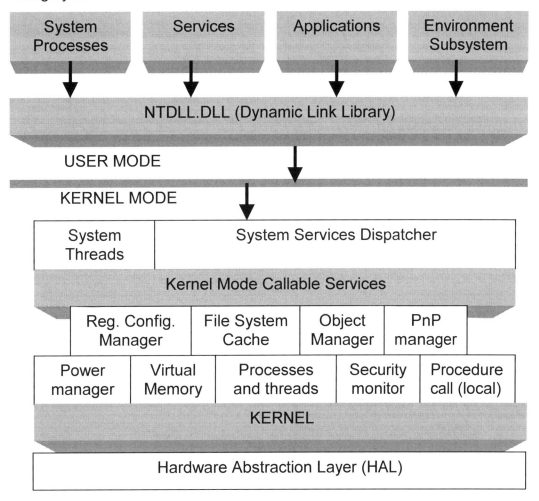

Figure 1.4. Simplified Windows NT 2000 Kernel Architecture [6]

Typically, a kernel includes an interrupt handler that looks after all requests or completed I/O operations, which compete for the kernel's services. It will also have a scheduler that determines which programs share the kernel's processing time and in what order. With reference to Figure 1.4, it is seen that all the processor services performed in kernel mode need to pass through the hardware abstraction layer (HAL) before accessing the hardware. The Windows HAL provides a link to the hardware interfaces such as buses, I/O devices, interrupts, interval timers, DMA, memory cache control etc. In the Windows O/S the HAL layer was first introduced with Windows 2000 O/S and for this reason drivers for devices pre-Windows 2000 are different to post-

Windows 2000. The introduction of the HAL layer implies that the O/S does not have direct access to the hardware and also, by suitably replacing the HAL, the O/S could run on different hardware platforms.

1.5. Windows NT memory model

As part of its 32-bit design, Windows NT contains two separate and distinct components that together comprise the core services of the NT operating system- the Windows NT Kernel and Executive. [6]

The Kernel works in conjunction with the Hardware Abstraction Layer (HAL), (see Figure 1.4) which gains its name from the fact that it provides a transition layer (i.e., it abstracts) between Windows NT's core operating system services and the actual hardware in use on the system (e.g., Intel, Alpha-based, uniprocessor, multiprocessor, etc.).

There are three key components responsible for the processing and memory management features provided by Windows NT operating system,

- **Virtual Memory Manager** (part of the Windows NT Executive) The Virtual Memory Manager maps virtual addresses in the process's address space to physical pages in computer memory. It hides the physical organisation of memory from the threads of the process in order to ensure that threads can access their own memory but not the memory of other processes. (Threads are sub-processes within a process).

- **Process Manager** (part of the Windows NT Executive) This part of the O/S creates and deletes processes and manages process and thread objects. It also provides a standard set of services for creating and using threads and processes in a particular subsystem environment.

- **Thread Dispatcher** (part of the Windows NT Kernel) Part of the NT Kernel responsible for scheduling the execution for threads. Threads can also be executed in a uniform way across all available processors, which is part of the Symmetric Multiprocessing (SMP) architecture of Windows NT and later versions.

13

Virtual DOS Machine (VDM)

The Disk Operating System (DOS) was 16-bit and all applications that were designed to run on this platform use the same 16-bit memory model. The 16 address bits enable access to an address of 64K locations (i.e. 2^{16}=64K). This is the size of the segment under DOS and corresponds to the Intel segmented memory model. DOS limitations were largely due to the size of these segments. Namely there are 16 possible segments all of the same size of 64K. This allows a total address space (using segmentation) of 16x64K= 1MB, which at the time in 1980 when the PC was designed, was a lot of memory. PCs and the MS-DOS operating system were designed to use the first 640 KB of RAM for programs and the operating system; this block of RAM is known as Conventional Memory. The Upper Memory space from 640 to 1024 KB was left for use by hardware devices such as graphics cards etc. Therefore only 640K of memory was available to accommodate the O/S and to execute programs. This imposed a limit on the size of program that could run in DOS.

Windows 95 was designed from scratch and departed from the DOS memory architecture. Nevertheless in order to maintain backward compatibility Windows 95 included a virtual DOS machine (VDM), which was designed to run all 16-bit applications. Since Windows 95 was 32-bit, these 16-bit applications all used a separate 16-bit address space. Thus a VDM was designed as a separate application to run DOS programs in their own memory. If more than one DOS application was activated to run in Windows 95, then they all shared the same 16-bit memory space. If the memory was corrupted by one application, it would fail that application and all others would fail at the same time. Managing VDM under Windows follows the same procedure as applies for any application that is running in Windows. It uses the Windows O/S and all the resources in the same way that any other application would, but the difference is that it runs in separate memory. Windows NT retains the VDM and this is also used to run the 16-bit applications.

1.6. Microprocessor Hardware

A microprocessor is a highly integrated chip that contains components like the CPU, memory, I/O ports, timers etc. Buses carry digital signals and are used to interconnect the various components. All computer operation is based on processing digital signals that have their values represented by a series of binary bits. Each bit is represented by one of two possible voltage levels, typically 0V and 5V d.c. (TTL). [7] For example, a voltage of around 5V can be used to represent a binary value of '1' and a voltage of 0V is used to represent a binary value of '0'.

In digital computers these binary values are processed by an arrangement of Boolean arithmetic operators. A series of these operations constitutes a computation. Thus, a microprocessor is an integrated circuit that contains all the digital circuits that are needed to perform the required data processing.

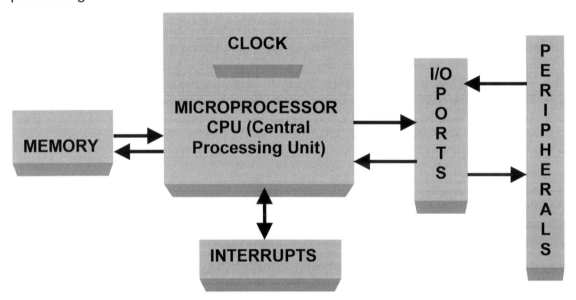

Figure 1.5. Standard computer components.

In order for a microprocessor to be useful it needs to connect to other digital components such as memory, input/output, clock etc. A typical arrangement of components as shown in Figure 1.5 would use a central clock that determines the standard clock rate for all CPU activity. For example, all instructions executed by the CPU are timed in terms of the number of clock cycles that they consume.

An interrupt system allows the microprocessor to be programmed to respond to external or internal events. Typically interrupts are vectored so that when they are triggered, and Interrupt Service Routine (ISR) is executed. Here, the term vectored means that the location of the ISR is provided when the interrupt occurs.

Buses connect the CPU to memory and input/output space so that data can be processed and transmitted to and from peripheral devices.

System Clock

Each operation involving the CPU and the system bus is synchronised by an internal clock, which runs at a constant frequency. The basic unit of time for machine instructions is a machine cycle (which is not always the same as the clock cycle). The length of a clock cycle is the time required for one complete clock pulse. Figure 1.6 shows how the clock cycle is timed.

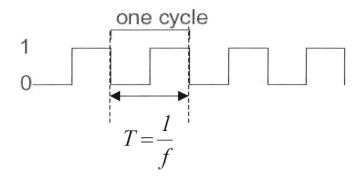

Figure 1.6. Clock cycle

The duration of a clock cycle is the reciprocal of the frequency of the CPU clock. For example, a clock with the frequency of $1GHz$ will have one clock cycle duration of $T = \dfrac{1}{1 \times 10^9} = 1nS$. Every instruction that is executed by the CPU takes up an integer number of clock cycles. For example on an 8086 CPU, an increment register instruction will take one clock cycle, an addition to the accumulator will take 10 clock cycles and an integer multiply instruction will take approximately 100 clock cycles.

Some instructions may require access to peripheral devices and since these are relatively slow, accessing them cannot happen at CPU clock speed. To accommodate this speed difference special architecture arrangements are designed. For example a hierarchy of buses running at different speeds with interconnecting bridges can accommodate speed differential between components. This will be discussed in Chapter 4 of this text. Additionally, instructions requiring frequent memory access have empty clock cycles which are called wait states because of the difference between the speeds of the CPU, the system bus, and memory circuits.

Interrupts

An interrupt is the term used to signify an interruption of the sequential execution of the microprocessor programme. An interrupt can be software or hardware generated and will stop the execution of the programme when it occurs. What happens after the programme is stopped depends on the nature of the interrupt and the associated interrupt service routine (ISR). For example, when no interrupts are used, if a programme sends a character to a printer to be printed out, then the CPU has nothing to do but wait until the printer is finished. With an interrupt the CPU can send the character to the printer and go on to do other things that are needed. When the printer has finished printing the character it will send an interrupt to the CPU to tell it that it is ready for another character. The CPU will respond to this interrupt by sending the next character and going back to its original business.

Often several interrupting devices will need servicing by the CPU and consequently interrupts are often prioritised. When two or more interrupts occur simultaneously, the one with the higher priority will be executed first.

Central Processing Unit (CPU)

The CPU performs numerical processing (addition, subtraction), logical operations and timing functions. It controls the overall operation of the system through a set of instructions programmed in memory. This programme is stored in non-volatile memory and is often termed micro-code (or micro-programme). Also this level of programming is sometimes termed firmware (as opposed to software and hardware). In general the CPU operates by reading data and control signals from memory or I/O device, executing one instruction at a time and sending data and control signals to the outside world through the output port.

To perform this task all CPUs contain an Arithmetic and Logic Unit (ALU), a Control Unit (CU) and registers along with control circuitry to interconnect these, as shown in Figure 1.7.

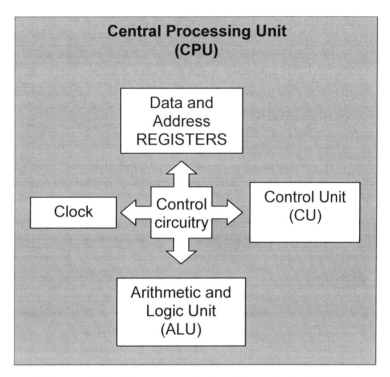

Figure 1.7. Components inside a typical CPU

The ALU contains a digital adder circuit to perform binary arithmetic (some will also contain multiplication and division), and logic and data shifting operations. The ALU also contains flag bits that signal the result of arithmetic and logical operations such as sign, zero, and carry and parity information.

Registers provide temporary storage within the CPU for memory addresses, status words etc. Each register is a set of flip-flops (FF) with each FF representing one bit (i.e. 8 bits = byte, 2 bytes=16 bits = word, 2 words= 32 bits = double word). The width of the data bus determines the actual number of FFs that are used. These FFs are active devices, based on transistor circuits and they provide the fastest level of memory available. However, because they are active devices, they consume power and also take up physical space on the CPU integrated circuit (IC). This means that the number of registers that can be included within the IC is constrained by chip size and heat dissipation of the housing. Some general aspects of digital circuits including D-Type flip-flops are included in Appendix 1.

The control circuitry coordinates all microprocessor activity. Using clock inputs, the required sequence of events is maintained for the processing task. The control circuitry decodes the instruction bits and issues control signals to units inside the CPU and those outside it, to perform the processing action.

In Chapter 5 we will look at how the program is executed inside the CPU and this will also include reference to the internal registers and also the control unit (CU).

Memory

In computer systems the two most common types of memory are random access memory (RAM) and read only memory (ROM).

RAM: Random access means that we can read and write to memory. This memory is volatile (i.e. it will lose its contents when the supply is switched off) and it can be either Static (SRAM) or Dynamic (DRAM). Static RAM stores a bit of information in a FF as with registers mentioned earlier, it is asynchronous, it does not require a clock and its contents remain intact while the supply power is available. Dynamic RAM stores a bit of information as a charge. It uses the gate-substrate capacitance of a MOS transistor as an elementary memory cell. The obvious advantage is that it is smaller than a FF and consequently DRAMs have a high memory density and they are slower and cheaper than SRAMs. Their main disadvantage is that the charge will leak and the memory will lose its charge after a few milliseconds. To prevent loss of data DRAMs are refreshed every millisecond by reading from it and writing back to it. This will be performed on blocks of memory rather than single memory locations.

VRAM: Video RAM memory is specifically designed for use in video systems. The fundamental difference between VRAM and standard DRAM is that VRAM is dual-ported. This means that it has two access paths, and can be written to and read from simultaneously. This is particularly useful in video operations where a new screen image is calculated, written to memory, and sent to the monitor many times per second. Dual porting allows these operations to occur at the same time (i.e. concurrently).

VRAM provides substantially more bandwidth than standard DRAM. However, VRAM is more complex and requires more silicon per bit than standard DRAM, which means that it is more expensive. [8]

ROM: as the name implies this type of memory can only be read from. Once the memory is filled (programmed) with information this remains unchanged even if power is switched off. Five main types of ROM exist,

- Masked ROM,
- Programmable ROM (PROM),
- Erasable PROM (EPROM),
- Electrically Erasable PROM (EEPROM or E^{2}PROM) and Flash ROM

Masked ROM: This is mask programmed by the manufacturer. The information stored in this type of memory is supplied as a bit pattern and the manufacturer makes the necessary connection mask for the production of the ROM. In view of the cost of producing a mask this type of ROM is usually subject to minimum quantity (i.e. minimum 1000 ROMs) and are therefore intended for large production volumes.

PROM: This is read only memory, which can be programmed directly by the user, using a special PROM Programmer. The user can program the required bit pattern but once this is done no changes can be made and the PROM becomes very much like ROM. Because it is not mask-programmed it is cheaper than ROM and for most systems requiring 10-100s units it is the preferred alternative.

Erasable PROM (EPROM). These are read only memories programmable by the user which can be reprogrammed a number of times using a programmer and an eraser. Several technologies are used to implement EPROMs. Once programmed, an EPROM will retain its charge for a number of years. They are easily erased by exposure to ultra-violet light. For this reason EPROM chips have a quartz window that lets in UV light. This window is usually covered with an opaque tape after the memory has been programmed so that it is not inadvertently exposed to UV light.

Electrically Erasable Programmable Read Only Memory (E2PROM). This type of memory can be read from and written to. The disadvantage is that writing to it requires a relatively long time (i.e. one millisecond) while the read operation can be done in a microsecond. It is therefore not suitable as a general-purpose read/write memory. In addition, it uses complex technologies resulting in low density and the necessity for multiple voltages. Typically, EEPROM will be used where it is necessary to store a small number of parameters infrequently. Its advantage is that it is non-volatile. Flash programmable ROMs are also electrically erasable and are becoming increasingly common in embedded applications. The main difference between E2PROM and Flash devices is that flash technology cannot erase individual bytes. It can only be erased one sector at a time with typical sector sizes in the range of 256 bytes to 16KB. This is not a major disadvantage since in embedded applications it is often necessary to erase blocks of memory.

Direct Memory Access (DMA)

From the standpoint of execution speed the efficiency of a microprocessor can be improved by using direct memory access. In ordinary I/O operations, the CPU supervises the entire data transfer as it executes I/O instructions to transfer data from the input device to the CPU and then from the CPU to the specified memory location. Similarly, data going from memory to the output device goes via the CPU. Some peripheral devices transfer information to and from memory faster than the CPU can accomplish the transfer under program control. By using DMA, the CPU allows the peripheral device to hold and control the bus, transferring the data directly to and from memory without involving the CPU. When the DMA transfer is completed, the peripheral device removes the hold request signal and thereby releases the bus to the CPU. In order to enable DMA transfer a DMA controller (DMAC) is provided. A DMAC implements the transfer algorithm in hardware, which is much faster than would be possible in software. It therefore automates data transfer between memory and I/O device.

Input-Output devices

These are also called peripherals, and they provide the means by which the CPU communicates with the outside world. In a typical microcomputer system output devices are controlled via the output ports. These can be serial (RS232) or parallel ports (i.e. printer port). Parallel ports are 8-bits wide or multiples thereof. These ports are attached to output devices via a port controller chip. In serial communication this chip is termed the USART (Universal Synchronous Transmitter Receiver), which means that it can receive and transmit asynchronous and synchronous data. No such standard is available for parallel communication. Intel for example use the term Programmable Input - Output (PIO) for the interface chip, Motorola use PIA, Rockwell use PDC etc. The essential function of these chips whatever the term used is to provide a basic input and output interface for 8-bits of parallel data. In addition the chip is programmable which means that it can be programmed to operate in a selection of modes. I/O communication is done over dedicated I/O buses and these are discussed in Chapter 4.

1.7. Data, Address and Control buses

For communication over buses to be effective the system needs to know when the byte of information is sent and to which device. In other words in order to send information to a device some information is required on its whereabouts and the address bus provides this information. The address bus therefore provides a unique address that corresponds to one of the memory or I/O elements of the system.

The control bus carries the control signals to the memory or I/O devices specifying when this is done and in which direction i.e. from the CPU to the device or the reverse.

As mentioned earlier the term architecture can refer to either hardware or software, or to a combination of these two. Hardware computer architecture generally consists of components such as the CPU, memory and Input/Output devices. These hardware architecture components are interconnected by a number of single line sets, called buses as shown in Figure 1.8. Typically three buses are present and these are the Data, Control and Address buses. The data bus is used to transfer data between the connected units. The width of the data bus in modern CPUs is typically 32 or 64 bits, which, at any instant, represents a 32 or 64 bit binary value. A wider bus can transfer data faster and hence would be desirable in the interests of overall computer speed. The address bus is used to specify the source or destination of data. The control bus is used to transmit timing and control signals between modules. Chapter 5 considers buses in more detail.

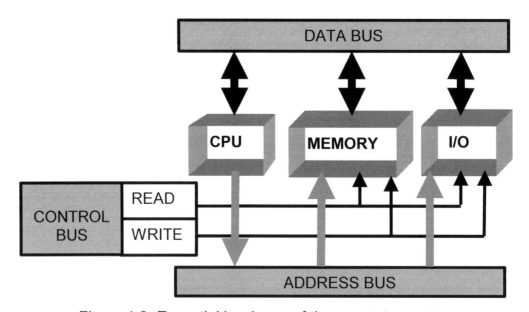

Figure 1.8. Essential hardware of the computer system

Buses are essentially a group of conductors, which carry electrical signals between components. The CPU itself, as a chip will have an internal architecture that will include buses. Outside the CPU, devices on the motherboard connected to the CPU will also have buses that connect them. Thus it is seen that buses can be implemented at different hardware levels.

1.8. Standard computer architecture

An important way to differentiate between internal processor architectures is by counting the number of buses used to communicate between the systems registers and its arithmetic and logic unit (ALU). For convenience and in order to illustrate this process we will use the example of the standard Intel 80x88 architecture as shown in Figure 1.9.

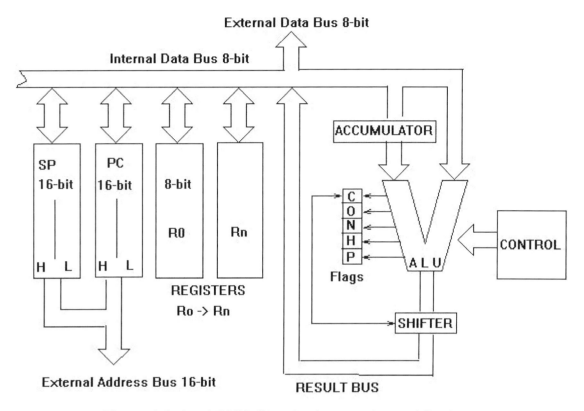

Figure 1.9. Intel 8088 Standard computer architecture

This is a single bus, accumulator based architecture, which makes efficient use of the chip area. A special accumulator register is added to one of the inputs to the ALU. The control box to the right of Figure 1.9 represents the control unit, which synchronises the operation of the entire system. It generates synchronisation signals between the ALU, the I/O and memory. It decodes, fetches and executes instructions. The control unit also manages the control bus. The sequencing of the control unit is performed by an internal specialised program called the micro program, which is stored in ROM and is normally not accessible to the user. (See Chapter 5) Figure 1.9 also shows a number of flags associated with the ALU and the shifter operation. These will be described next.

Shifting operations

Shifting operation is performed on a byte. 8-bits form a byte and in binary arithmetic each bit is a power of 2 as shown in Table 1.3. When bits are manipulated for arithmetic and logic operations the result can cause overflow, zero, negative or other situations, which are monitored by a series of flags. Each one of these flags is either High or Low (i.e. On or OFF) to indicate whether the operation has caused the state of the flag to occur.

Table 1.3

(MSB)   (LSB)

128	64	32	16	8	4	2	1
2^7	2^6	2^5	2^4	2^3	2^2	2^1	2^0
0	1	1	0	1	0	1	1

Where (MSB) - most significant bit, (LSB) - Least significant bit.

The binary byte 01101011 shown in Table 1.3 has a decimal equivalent of:

$0+64+32+0+8+0+2+1=107$

If for example the above byte were shifted to the left by one bit (i.e. each bit is shifted one position to the left) the new byte would be,

128	64	32	16	8	4	2	1
2^7	2^6	2^5	2^4	2^3	2^2	2^1	2^0
1	1	0	1	0	1	1	0

The new binary byte 11010110 has a decimal equivalent of $128+64+0+0+16+0+4+2+0=214$, i.e., the number has doubled. Shifting operations are the quickest means of multiplication and division by a factor of 2. i.e. divide by 32 will be the same as shifting five bits to the right.

In a regular shift the bit coming in on the right of the byte is always zero. The bit falling off the left side following a shift is captured in a special "status register" where it is stored in order that it can be tested. In this context the bit that falls off the left is the carry bit and its status is held in the carry flag. The carry flag also monitors the overflow in arithmetic operations. For example if the two bytes above were added together the eighth bit would carry a '1' as the ninth bit which would be stored in the carry flag. This is shown in Table 1.4

Table 1.4

128	64	32	16	8	4	2	1
2^7	2^6	2^5	2^4	2^3	2^2	2^1	2^0
1	1	1	1	1	1	0	0

+

1	0	0	0	0	0	0	0

=

1	0	1	1	1	1	1	0	0

Carry bit

Thus the overflow of the 8-bit result generates a carry i.e. the ninth-bit.

Flags

Other flags used are as follows,

Overflow (O): Overflow denotes the fact that an arithmetic carry within the word has modified the value of the most significant bit (MSB), resulting in a sign error in the case of a 2's compliment notation.

Note: Bit 7 (the MSB) in 2's compliment notation indicates the sign of the number (i.e. positive if 0 negative if 1). Thus, whenever 2's compliment addition is performed the result can inadvertently change the 7th bit and consequently cause an error by changing a positive into a negative number.

In order to monitor this occurrence an Overflow flag is provided so that corrective action can be taken. Mathematically, the overflow is the exclusive OR (XOR) of the carry bit out of bit 7 and the carry generated from bit 6 to bit 7. The overflow will normally be used only when performing 2's complement arithmetic.

Negative (or sign flag) (N or S): The N bit is directly connected to bit 7 (MSB) of the result and indicates whether the result is positive or negative.

Zero (Z): The Z bit is set whenever the result of an operation is zero. It is used by arithmetic instructions to determine whether the result is zero and also by logic operations such as compare. Whenever the result of a comparison is successful, the Z bit is set to 1. This is because the compare operation implements a logical XOR between the word being tested and the pattern to which it is being compared. (Note that XOR output is zero when inputs are the same and one when inputs differ.)

Parity (P): This bit is not always present in microprocessors but when it is, it is used to test whether data has been transmitted correctly. The principle of parity is to count the number of 1's present in 8 bits. If this number is even then parity is even and conversely when it is odd. The parity test is used in communications and is not normally supplied in the microprocessor since it is usually implemented in a UART. Nonetheless, an even parity scheme will complete the number of 1's of a 7-bit word by adding either a 0 or a 1 so that the total number of 1's is even. Conversely, an odd parity scheme will set the eighth bit so that the total number of 1's is odd. The parity flag is used to detect whether the parity count is correct or not. Assuming for example even parity, the parity bit will be set whenever the number of bits within a word is not even, indicating parity error. The parity bit is an extra bit (bit 8) appended to the data and does not affect the value of the data.

Note: A byte has eight bits starting from bit 0 and going to bit 7. The MSB is therefore bit 7 and not bit 8. Other status bits can be provided within the flags register. In particular the interrupt enable bit may be provided. Whenever this bit is set, outside interrupts will be accepted and conversely when it is not set (i.e. cleared) external interrupts will be inhibited, in other words they are said to be masked.

Address registers

To the left of Figure 1.9 are two registers connected to data bus on the top and the address bus on the bottom. These are address registers intended for storage of addresses. They are 16-bit which means they are made up of two bytes a high byte (H) and a low byte (L). In this arrangement the only way to load an address register is via the data bus. Two bytes, the high and the low byte, need to be transferred for a 16-bit address. The low byte represents bits $0 \rightarrow 7$ and the High byte bits $8 \rightarrow 15$. At least two address registers are present in most microprocessors. In Figure 1.9 these are shown as the Stack Pointer (SP) and the Program Counter (PC) registers.

Program Counter (PC): The program counter register must be present in any microprocessor. In contains the address of the next instruction to be executed. Being as the execution of the program is sequential the microprocessor must always know the address of the next instruction to be executed. In order that this instruction can be executed the memory address of its location needs to be supplied to the microprocessor. This address is stored in the program counter and is deposited on the address bus when the next instruction is to be fetched for execution. This instruction will normally reside in memory and once it has been located its contents will be sent from memory to the CPU for execution. The contents of this location are the instruction for the microprocessor to execute.

Stack pointer (SP): The stack pointer points to the top of the stack, which is an area in memory that is reserved for storing important information during the execution of a program. For example, when an interrupt occurs, the stack will be loaded with the location of the current instruction being executed. Every microprocessor must have an area in memory (RAM)) that it can use as the stack. In order to keep track of the top of the stack a stack pointer register is used. The stack is a 'Last In First Out' structure shown in Figure 1.10. It is a chronological structure, which accumulates events in the order in which they are deposited. The oldest event placed on the stack is at the bottom and it is the last to come off it. As shown in Figure 1.10 events or symbols are placed onto the stack with a PUSH command and taken off it with a POP command.

Stacks can be implemented in software or hardware. Software stacks are cheaper and slower than hardware stacks. It is possible to provide a hardware stack by dedicating it a set of internal registers to implement the stack. This is limited in size mainly due to cost and a software stack is often the preferred alternative.

In software stacks the stack is implemented in microprocessor RAM. The base of the stack is selected by the programmer and is managed automatically within the SP register. The SP usually points to the first available word on the stack in order to provide the fastest PUSH and PULL operations possible. The stack is particularly useful in interrupts when the important information of the executing programme is PUSHed onto the stack to be saved before control is switched to the interrupt service routine. When the programme is resumed the contents of the stack are POPed back. It is up to the programmer to decide what information needs to be PUSHed and POPed when an interrupt occurs.

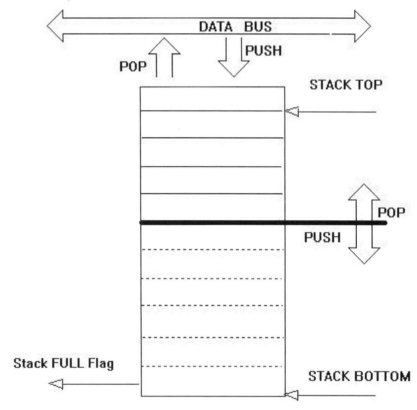

Figure 1.10. The Stack is accessed with PUSH and POP instructions

Stack programming is an additional useful feature of stacks. Since the PUSH and POP instructions are very fast, stack programming is used to load words onto the bus that are pushed and popped in a prescribed sequence to be executed as a program.

Exercises

1.1. How do you define the term computer architecture?

1.2. Describe the basic components of computer architecture.

1.3. Discuss the relationship between hardware and software architectures for a computer system.

1.4. Discuss the different levels of programming that an O/S typically supports.

1.5. If you wrote a 16-bit DOS application and you want to run it in a Windows NT DOS window (i.e. Virtual Dos Machine), would it use the Windows NT O/S to run? If so why?

1.6. If you wanted to write a kernel for a general purpose CPU (i.e. Intel 8086), which programming language would you use and why?

1.7. If you designed a program to simulate the flight of an aircraft and you wanted this to run under windows NT platform, would you need to use the Windows API, if so why?

1.8. Explain the essential functions of a computer operating system.

1.9. Discuss the different types of operating systems and their typical applications. Distinguish between general purpose and real-time O/Ss and give some examples of each.

1.10. Explain the Windows NT internal kernel architecture.

1.11. Within the NT kernel architecture, explain the memory management component.

1.12. Describe the basic components of a CPU.

1.13. Why are shifter operations useful with registers?

1.14. Describe the typical flags and what they are used for in the CPU.

1.15. Explain the basic functions of address registers.

1.16. What is a Stack used for and how can it be implemented in a computer system.

CHAPTER 2 PROCESS MANAGEMENT

2.1. Introduction

In computer processing terms a process refers to an execution of a program and is used as a unit of measure of CPU activity. In a multitasking operating system, the Central Processing Unit (CPU) has to manage several processes simultaneously. In reality a single CPU can only execute one instruction at a time. Nevertheless, a number of processes can be loaded into memory, and the CPU can switch between them and execute each of these for a short amount of time. The O/S determines the actual length of time spent on each process, and the term that is often used to describe it is the 'quantum'. The actual changeover of the CPU executing one process and changing over to another is generally referred to as context switch.

With modern CPUs running at clock speeds of above 1GHz, these context switches can occur very frequently, and therefore they are transparent to the user. Thus, by switching rapidly between processes a CPU can multitask, even if it is only capable of executing one instruction at a time.

Related to multitasking is the unit of measure for the clock speeds of microprocessors (for example, clock frequency of 1GHz). The clock period at this frequency is,

$$\frac{1}{1\times10^9} = 1nS \qquad (2.1)$$

For example, if a task is allocated 10 ms of CPU time (i.e. quantum) the number of CPU clock cycles that will be allocated to this task is one million clocks, which is calculated as follows,

$$\frac{1\times10^{-3}}{1\times10^{-9}} = 1\times10^6$$

In order to give a measure of the relative processing potential it is useful to note that the Intel x86 family of CPUs will perform a simple integer addition in approximately 10 clock cycles. Which means that at 1GHz clock speeds, 100,000 of these can be performed in 10 ms. i.e.

$$\frac{1 \times 10^6}{10} = 1 \times 10^5$$

This means that the task execution time is unnoticeable to human reflexes and therefore multitasking is transparent to the human operator.

2.2. Time-sharing operation

A time-shared operating system uses CPU scheduling to provide each user with a small portion of a time-shared computer. Since all programs that are executing need to be in RAM, each user has a separate program in memory. When a program executes, it uses the CPU for only a short time before it either finishes or needs to perform I/O. I/O may also be interactive; that is, output to a display, or input from a keyboard, which in real terms can take a large number of CPU clocks to wait for an event to complete. For example the speed of a human operator typing a character on a keyboard may be in the region of five characters per second. In other words it takes a human operator 200mS to type each character on the keyboard.

To accept the character from the keyboard, the CPU will execute an interrupt and do some processing. Let us assume that this takes the CPU 50µS to execute. This means that the CPU will work for 50µS and then wait for 200mS until the next character is received from the keyboard. In other words the CPU is working $\frac{50 \times 10^{-6}}{200 \times 10^{-3}} \times 100 = 0.025\%$ of time and wasting 99.975% of its available processing time. Rather than let the CPU wait idle when this happens, the operating system will rapidly switch the CPU to another process. A software program called the scheduler performs this task.

Time-sharing operating systems provide a mechanism for concurrent execution of several processes, which must be simultaneously present in memory. In order to facilitate this some form of memory management is required for memory protection, and also to assist with CPU scheduling. So that a reasonable response time can be obtained, jobs may have to be swapped in and out of main memory. Hence, disk management must also be provided. Time-sharing systems must also provide an on-line file system and memory protection mechanisms. This is particularly important in situations when several copies of the same program are in memory (RAM) at the same time. This can occur when one program may be under execution more than once or several users may be running the same program simultaneously. An example could be a compiler, which would appear to be compiling several different programs simultaneously.

A program executing in this manner is called a re-entrant. Machine code of the program that is in memory must not be altered during execution and therefore separate memory must be maintained for each execution. In this manner, each copy of the program that is executing is a unique process.

2.3. Multithreading

The basic principle of program execution is the Fetch-Execute cycle, where the CPU reads (fetches) the machine instruction from memory and executes it. This is repeated for every instruction in sequence until the program completes. When execution of a process begins the O/S creates a data structure called Process Control Board (PCB), which serves to control the process. Within the PCB is a process identification number that is used as an identifier during scheduling.

A thread, also called a lightweight process, is a sub-process that behaves as a stand-alone subsection of the process. A simple way to view a thread is as an independent program counter within a process, indicating the position of the instruction that the thread is working on. Almost all modern operating systems support the concept of threads by allowing multiple threads in a single process, which is referred to as multithreading.

- MS-DOS supports a single user process and a single thread.
- Some traditional UNIX systems are multiprogramming systems, thus support multiple user processes but only one execution path is allowed for each process.
- A Java Virtual Machine (JVM) is an example of a system of one process with multiple threads.
- Most modern operating systems, such as Windows, Solaris, Linux, and OS/2, support multithreading.

The advantage of using threads is that if the computer has many processors that support multi-threading, then threads can be distributed to different processors. In this case threads rather than processes form the basic unit of scheduling and execution. This makes the processing task more efficient in terms of system's overheads.

For example, in multithreading, the process which is executing would typically consist of many threads. In this case each of these threads shares the same address space and as a result of this, communication between threads is simple and efficient. If the O/S does not support multi-threading then processes are executed in their own address space. Consequently, inter-process communications involves additional mechanisms such as sockets or pipes. Thus, it is seen that the benefits of a multithreading derive from the conservation of resources. Since threads share the same code section, data section and O/S resources, less overall resources are used.

2.4. Clustering

In process execution terms, clustering can be considered the inverse of multitasking. A cluster is a group of independent processors that are used to execute portions of one common task. A task that needs to be executed is distributed across a cluster of processors, each of which executes a section of the task concurrently. The basic idea is shown in Figure 2.1, where to the left of the figure, a single CPU is distributing its resources across a number of processes that are executing concurrently (i.e. multitasking). On the right of the figure, a single process can be distributed across a number of CPUs (i.e. clustering). It needs to be said that either of these approaches can be expanded such that for example, multitasking can be arranged so that many CPUs work in a multi-processing configuration. This however does not mean that they are clustered. Similarly, many processes can be distributed across a cluster. Executing a process in this way requires some additional processing. For example, a network is used to provide inter-processor communication. Applications that are distributed across the processors of the cluster use either message passing or network shared memory for communication.

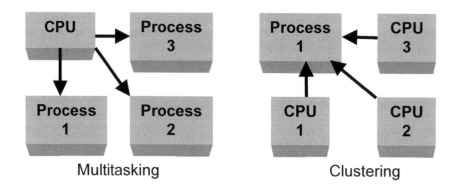

Multitasking   Clustering

Figure 2.1. Simplified view of multitasking and clustering

With the depreciating cost of Intel-based PCs, network clusters can be built relatively economically. Using PCs with large memories and connecting them into a high-performance network, with some additional clustering software, can provide significant computing power. For example, Windows Compute Cluster Server 2003 [9] supports five different cluster topologies. These clusters can use Public, Private, and Message Passing Interface (MPI) networks.

Public network: Here cluster traffic is shared with other organisational functions. All intra-cluster management and deployment traffic is carried on the public network. Cluster performance is therefore degraded.

Private network: A dedicated network carries intra-cluster communication between nodes. This network, if it exists, carries management, deployment, and MPI traffic. This provides significant improvement in cluster performance, but it is more expensive than the public network option.

Message Passing Interface (MPI) network: Message passing interface networks are dedicated, high bandwidth and low latency networks that carry parallel MPI communication between cluster nodes. Of the three networks listed here, this is the highest bandwidth network. Some examples of high-speed networks include,

- Gigabit Ethernet.
- 10-Gigabit Ethernet.
- Myrinet©. [10]

Clustering is most widely recognised, as the ability to combine multiple systems in such a way that they provide services which a single system could not. It is used to achieve higher availability, scalability (allows expansion of systems) and easier management. Clusters are designed for improved performance by distributing the computational workload across an array of hosts. For the cluster to be effective, these hosts must communicate over high-data-rate and low-latency networks. Another feature of clusters is their availability and consequently clustering solutions are described according to their ability to withstand faults. That is to say, a high availability cluster would allow a computation to continue with a subset of hosts. The inter-processor communications architecture would detect and isolate faults by providing alternative communication paths. More discussions of clusters will be covered in Chapter 7 in the context of parallel computing.

2.5. Scheduling

In a multi-tasking environment, the operating system has the job of determining the sequence and timing of the execution of processes. Schedulers that adhere to prescribed scheduling policies do this. Process scheduling is divided into three levels,

- **High-Level** (or long term or job scheduling): Deals with decisions as to whether to admit a new job to the system. All jobs enter the system into the READY queue. (See Figure 2.2)

- **Medium-Level**: Decides whether to temporarily remove a process from the system or to re-introduce the process (i.e. to balance processor loading).

- **Low-Level** (short-term or processor scheduling): Decides which ready process to assign to the CPU.

In order to maintain consistency schedulers work according to a prescribed policy, such as for example (First Come First Serve (FCFS), Shortest Job First (SJF) etc). Time slicing is often applied with scheduling policies in order to allocate a prescribed period of CPU time to a task. For example, in a time-slicing environment the kernel may interrupt each process after a few milliseconds to switch control to another process. Schedulers that work at different levels have different tasks, but in a general sense, the objectives of scheduling are as follows,

- Provide maximum process throughput.
- Allocate jobs to the processor according to a policy. This way the processes are treated consistently.
- During busy periods, in order to prevent CPU over-load, it should avoid further loading (e.g. inhibit any new job or new users) or reduce level of service (i.e. response time).

Scheduling levels

In order to better describe the various levels of scheduling it is necessary to introduce the three state and five state process models. These models describe the states that a process can take during execution. The assumption here is that a single processor executes all the tasks. In a multitasking environment, where more than one task is being processed by a single CPU, it follows that tasks need to be in different states of execution. The three state diagram identifies the three states that a process can have as ready, running and blocked. The five state models allow the blocked and ready states to be suspended, and therefore these are added to the basic three states. (See Figure 2.3)

Three state diagram

In a multitasking environment each of the many processes can be in one of three distinct states. These are the ready, blocked and running states as shown in Figure 2.2. A process traverses between these states under the control of schedulers.

With reference to Figure 2.2, it is seen that a process enters the system via the High Level Scheduler (HLS) and enters the READY state. There may be a queue of processes in this state and in this case they are maintained in a linked list of their respective PCBs. (process control blocks)

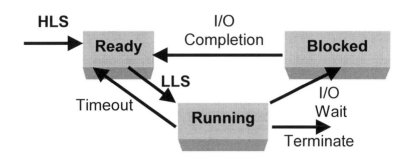

Figure 2.2. Three state diagram

When the CPU is free to accept a process, it is the job of the Low Level Scheduler (LLS) to determine which of the processes that are in the READY queue, should be allocated to the CPU. The process that is in the running state can exit that state in one of three ways. Namely, it can terminate or the scheduler can time it out in which case it is returned to the READY queue. It can also leave the running state if it enters an I/O wait and in this case the LLS sends the process into the BLOCKED state. If the process goes into a BLOCKED state then the LLS will place the next process in the READY queue into the RUNNING state. When the I/O wait for the BLOCKED process is complete, it is placed by the LLS into the READY state and its PCB joins the linked list queue.

Five state diagram

The five-state model arises from the operations of the Medium Level Scheduler (MLS) where a process that is in READY, BLOCKED or RUNNING state can be SUSPENDED. This gives rise to two more states namely, the READY SUSPENDED and BLOCKED SUSPENDED states. The reason to temporarily suspend a state can arise from a number of O/S related actions. For example, a timer interrupt would cause the CPU to suspend the currently executing process in order to pass control onto an interrupt service routine (ISR). When the ISR completes the process that was suspended can be resumed. However it has to be said that if the process was suspended from the running state, it cannot resume in that state and has to be returned to the READY queue. Therefore the transition from suspended state into running state is always through the ready state. This is because there is only one point of entry into the running state and this is from the READY queue.

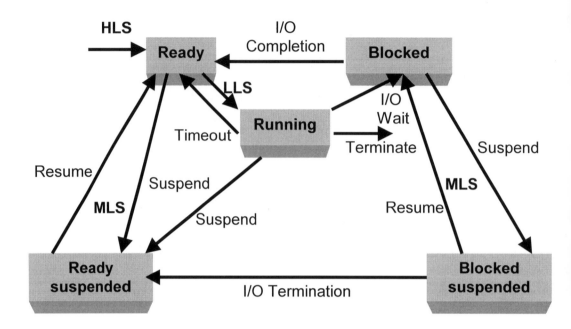

Figure 2.3. Five state diagram

A more detailed description of the three levels of scheduling is given next.

2.6. Scheduling Policies

Scheduling policies are the rules according to which a decision is made as to whether a particular action is taken. In process terminology the actions refer to processes, and so can range from suspending, resuming, loading a process etc. These policies are therefore used to decide how to schedule the activities of the different tasks in a multitasking environment. Scheduling policies are divided into two major categories, namely pre-emptive and non-pre-emptive depending on whether the processes can be interrupted or not.

Pre-emptive

In the pre-emptive scheme LLS may remove a process from a RUNNING state in order to allocate another process to the CPU. The cost of this in processing time is the added overhead of the context switching. Nevertheless, this may be justified in cases where a long process is in danger of monopolising the processor. Additionally, pre-emptive multitasking allows the computer system to more reliably guarantee each process a regular time-slice of CPU time.

Non-pre-emptive

A scheduling discipline is non-pre-emptive if, once a process has been allocated to the CPU, the CPU cannot be taken away from that process. The only time the process will relinquish the CPU is when it terminates, or when it enters the BLOCKED state. Another, more drastic way to leave the READY state is when a non-maskable interrupt (NMI) occurs. (i.e. power loss). In non-pre-emptive systems, response times are more predictable because incoming jobs cannot displace waiting jobs, even if they have higher priority.

Another type of policy that is no longer very common is the cooperative policy that was used in the Windows 3.1 multitasking O/S. Effectively this was cooperative multitasking since each application when running would periodically relinquish control back to Windows scheduler. The main disadvantage is in that if an error occurs and the application is unable to transfer control to the operating system, it may freeze the system.

As mentioned earlier, schedulers work according to a prescribed scheduling policy. There are 6 Low level scheduling policies that are most commonly applied to process scheduling, these are as follows,

- (SJF)   Shortest Job First.
- (FCFS)   First Come First Serve.
- (RR)   Round Robin.
- (SRT)   Shortest Remaining Time.
- (HRN)   Highest Response Ratio Next.
- (MFQ)   Multilevel feedback queue.

FCFS-First Come First Serve

This is a non-pre-emptive policy and consequently it favours long jobs over short jobs. This is because the waiting time to run time ratio is smaller for long jobs than for short jobs. Table 2.1 shows the typical ratios that can be expected with this policy. Here it is seen that the shortest job has the highest wait-to-run time ratio.

Table 2.1

Process	Estimated run-time (T_{ER})	Waiting time (T_W)	Ratio (T_W)/(T_{ER})
P1	10	0	0/10=0
P2	2	1	11/2=0.55
P3	1	13	13/1=13
P4	100	14	14/100=1.4

SJF – Shortest Job First

This is another non-pre-emptive policy and it works on the basis that it schedules the shortest jobs first, leaving the longer jobs for later. The assumption here is that once the short jobs have been completed, and no more are left, the longer jobs can proceed. This avoids delaying the short jobs by waiting for long ones to finish. With SJF if there are a large number of shorter job there is a risk that the longer job suffers longer waits, and therefore may result in job starvation. For SJF an estimated run time must be available for each process and could be supplied by Job control Language (JCL). Table 2.2 shows the typical ratios that can be expected with this policy. Here is seen that in comparison to the FCFS, all jobs have a lower wait-to-run-time ratio. However the highest ratio is for the longest job.

Table 2.2

Process	Order SJF	Estimated run-time (T_{ER})	Waiting time (T_W)	Ratio (T_W)/(T_{ER})
P1	P3	1	0	0/1=0
P2	P2	2	1	1/2=0.5
P3	P1	10	3	3/10=0.3
P4	P4	100	13	13/100=1.3

SRT-Short Remaining Time

This is a pre-emptive variation of SJF that uses a timeout to context switch between jobs. It uses a time stamp to monitor the length of jobs and schedules these according to the principle of Shortest Remaining Time (SRT) policy. With this policy the job with the shortest time to completion is processed first. Each job runs for the duration of the timeout and then a new calculation is done to determine which of the remaining jobs are the shortest. Table 2.3 shows an example of the performance of this policy. Although this policy has the overhead of keeping a time-stamp, it is seen to be fair to all jobs, and more importantly, it guarantees that no jobs will be starved of CPU time.

Table 2.3 SRT

Proces s	Time in Unit	Order of SJF	Units of time elapsed FROM START						
			1	2	3	4	<--- >	10	11
P1	10	3	10	10	10	9			0
P2	2	2	2	1	0	-			-
P3	1	1	0	-	-	-			-
P4	100	4	100	100	100	100			39

Highest Response Next (HRN)

HRN is also a pre-emptive policy derived from SJF, which has been modified to allow the longer jobs to have a chance to complete. Calculating a dynamic priority after each unit of execution time does this. It is based on a calculated priority value and the formula is as follows,

$$P = \frac{T_W + T_{RT}}{T_{RT}} \qquad (2.2)$$

Looking at equation 2.2 it is clear that P is never less than 1. For example, assume two processes P1 and P2 with run times of 5 and 10 units respectively have both been waiting for 1 unit time. Their priority values can be calculated from (2.1) as follows,

$$P_1 = \frac{T_W + T_{RT}}{T_{RT}} = \frac{1+5}{5} = 1.2 \text{ and } P_2 = \frac{T_W + T_{RT}}{T_{RT}} = \frac{1+10}{10} = 1.1$$

From the result it is seen that process P1 has a higher priority value and therefore takes precedence over P2.

Consider another example. Assume process P4 has a run time of 100 units and has been waiting for 12 units of time. At this time, another process P5, with a run time value of 10 units joins the queue. Another unit of time later, after P4 has waited for 13 units of time, P5 has been in the queue for 1 unit of time and it has a running time of 10 units of time. The priority calculation for P4 and P5 would be,

$$P_4 = \frac{T_W + T_{ER}}{T_{ER}} = \frac{13+100}{100} = 1.13 \text{ and } P_2 = \frac{T_W + T_{ER}}{T_{ER}} = \frac{1+10}{10} = 1.1$$

In this situation even though P4 is a long job the priority has moved up higher than P5, which has shorter running time but joins the queue later. Table 2.4 show the calculated priorities for a range of process lengths.

Table 2.4 HRN with the Priority calculated priority value

Process	Estimated run-time (T_{ER})	Waiting time (T_W)	Priority value (T_W+T_{ER}) /(T_{ER})
P1	10	0	10/10 =1
P2	2	10	12/2 =6
P3	1	12	13/1 =13
P4	100	13	113/100 =1.13

Round Robin

Round robin is a common scheduling scheme where processes are allocated the CPU in a rotating fashion with a timeout signalling the change form one process to the next. (See Figure 2.4) A process is selected from the ready queue in the first-in-first-out (FIFO) sequence. Processes are assigned a quantum of time to run on processor, which must not be exceeded. As soon as the time quantum has been exceeded, an interrupt occurs and the executing process is placed at the back of the FIFO queue. A hardware timer that generates an interrupt at pre-set intervals usually provides the time quantum. This policy is pre-emptive which only occurs at expiry of quantum time.

Perhaps the most significant feature of this policy is that it guarantees the completion of even the longest jobs. Since each process is allocated a quantum, and when this has expired, it moves to the back of the queue, every process remains in the queue until it has completed. Thus, for n processes in the queue and a fixed time quantum (Q), each process gets a proportion of CPU time given by,

$$P_{CPU} = \frac{1}{n}$$

This is allocated in chunks of at most Q time units at a time. It follows that no process waits longer than $T_W = (n-1) \times Q$ time units. The main disadvantage of this policy is the significant overheads because each quantum time generates a context switch.

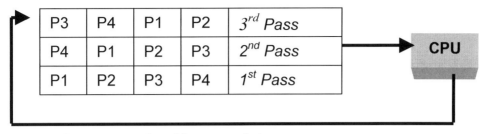

After a time slice "Quantum" the process
frees processor for next process

Figure 2.4. Round Robin Process scheduling

The choice of time quantum is very important with the round robin scheduling policy. It should not be too short because this will increase the frequency of context switch. Every context switch takes CPU time and this can lead to a condition called 'thrashing', where the CPU spends all its time context switching. On the other hand if the context switch is too long, that could introduce idle time, when the process has terminated and the quantum has not elapsed. (Typically quantum = 10-20 mS). Figure 2.4 represents round robin scheduling.

Multi-level feedback queues (MFQ)

MFQs are a combination of first in first out (FIFO) queues arranged at different higherarchical levels in accordance with the level of CPU usage. It combines serveral levels of FIFO queues with a time quantum applied to limit processor time given to each process. As the process runs, if it uses up its quantum, it will return to the back of the queue at the lower level and work its way back again. The highest level is for processes with the shortest CPU time and levels below this have progressively longer CPU time requirements. Transition from the higher level to the one below is achieved by providing a timeout (quantum Q). This is seen in Figure 2.5 which shows that a new process enters at the highest level, and progresses down the levels for as long as it does not complete.

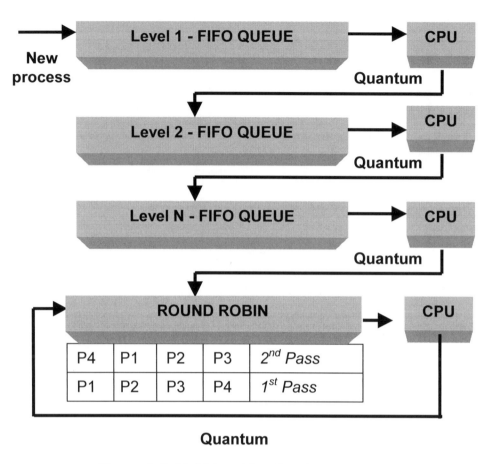

Figure 2.5. Multi-level feedback queues.

MFQs can be made adaptive by recording the level at which each process terminated when it was last in the queue. When the same process is next in the queue, instead of placing it at the highest level, it will be placed at the level that it exited. In this manner the process will not waste time in the higher levels where it will not complete. This is an attempt to provide an adaptive policy which treats processes on the basis of their past behaviour.

2.7. Scheduling parallel processes

Parallel processing refers to the execution of different processes at the same time. Parallel computers can be roughly classified according to the level at which the hardware supports parallelism. Multi-core and multi-processor computers having multiple processing elements within a single machine can be used to work on a multitude of tasks. On the other hand computer clusters, multi-programmable-multi-processors (MPPs), and grids use multiple computers to work on the same task. Specialised parallel computer architectures are sometimes used alongside traditional processors, for accelerating specific tasks. [11]

When you consider that processes executing in parallel will share resources, such as the CPU, memory and indeed sometimes they will share variables, then you are faced with a dilemma of how to ensure that the processing is executed accurately. This brings us to the issue of the various dependencies between processes. These can be data dependency where shared data is used and modifications to this data affect all the processes that use it. There are also issues of procedural dependency where procedures executed depend on the activities of another process. In systems that have a single CPU, parallel execution is possible by carefully scheduling execution of concurrent processes. This scheduling of processes to run at the same time is done on the principle that not all processes will require the use of a CPU throughout their execution. For example, a process may require an I/O call from a hard disk. This will take a significant proportion of time, and in this case the scheduler can release the CPU for use by another process until the I/O communication has been completed. (See the three-state and five-state state diagrams in the preceding section). With multiple CPUs the resources are still shared and even though a number of CPUs can execute independently, these dependencies restrict the level of parallel operation that can be achieved.

Another type of process that is used in computing is the sequential process. This kind of process differs from a parallel process in that it must execute sequentially. In other words the process executes as a sequence of instructions that must be performed in the particular order. In a multitasking environment it is therefore common to expect parallel scheduling implementations to include sequential as well as parallel processes. An abundance of literature is available on this subject and the paper by Zhou et al [12] provides a clear and concise description of effective scheduling in a mixed parallel and sequential processing environment. You are encouraged to read this paper, but for purposes of identifying some of the issues that are relevant I am providing a brief summary next.

Two level scheduling

(My summary of the paper)

The trend of parallel computer developments is towards networks consisting of a number of scalable parallel systems. In this type of system each processor, having a high-speed processing element, a large-size memory space and full functionality of a standard operating system, can operate as a stand-alone workstation for sequential computing. When interconnected by a high bandwidth and low-latency network, these processors can also be used for parallel computing. Therefore, the system provides a mixed parallel and sequential computing environment. This approach is scalable because it can adapt to increased demands. For example, a scalable network system would be one that can start with just a few nodes but can easily expand to thousands of nodes.

To efficiently utilize the system resources, it is very important to design an effective scheduling algorithm for mixed parallel and sequential workloads. There exist many scheduling schemes for parallel machines. The simplest and most commonly used method is batch job system. This system only allows one parallel program to run at a time. Once a parallel job enters the service, it will continuously be serviced until finished and all other parallel jobs have to wait in a batch queue outside of the system.

To solve problems encountered by the simple batch scheme, multiprogramming should be considered. Multiprogramming on parallel systems is much more complicated than that on sequential machines. We need to consider the problem of time-sharing, that is, the problem of interactive use of processors by many jobs simultaneously. We should also consider the problem of space sharing, that is, the problem of static/dynamic allocation of processors to different jobs. Scheduling schemes for time-sharing of a parallel system may be classified into two basic types. Namely,

1. **Local scheduling**. With local scheduling there is only a single queue in each processor. Except for higher (or lower) priorities being given, processes associated with parallel jobs are not distinguished from those associated with sequential jobs. The method simply

relies on existing local schedulers on each processor to schedule parallel jobs. Thus there is no guarantee that the processes belonging to the same parallel jobs can be executed at the same time across the processors. When many parallel programs are simultaneously running on a system, processes belonging to different jobs will compete for resources with each other and then some processes have to be blocked when communicating or synchronising with non-scheduled processes on other processors. This effect can lead to a significant degradation in overall system performance. One method to alleviate this problem is to use two phase blocking which is also referred to as implicit co scheduling. In this method a process waiting for communication spins for some time in the hope that the process to be communicated with on the other processor is also scheduled, and then blocks if the response is still not received. The reported experimental results indicate that for parallel workloads this scheduling scheme performs better than the simple local scheduling. However, one problem associated with local scheduling is that the scheduling of parallel jobs is independent of their service times. Thus the performance is unpredictable. If the system is busy, for example, short jobs may not be completed quickly.

2.   **Co-scheduling**: Using this method a number of parallel programs are allowed to enter a service queue. The processes of the same job will run simultaneously across the processors for only certain amount of time, which is called a scheduling slot. When a scheduling slot is ended, the processors will context-switch at the same time to give the service to processes of another job. All programs in the service queue take turns to receive the service in a coordinated manner across the processors. Thus programs never interfere with each other and short jobs are likely to be completed more quickly. There are however certain drawbacks associated with co scheduling. A significant one is that it is designed only for parallel

workloads. In each scheduling slot there is only one process running on each processor and the process simply does busy-waiting during communication/synchronisation. This will waste processor cycles and decrease the efficiency of processor utilisation.

It can be seen from the above discussion that both local scheduling and co scheduling have problems when scheduling mixed parallel and sequential workloads on scalable parallel computers.

The authors of the paper describe a two-level scheduling scheme for mixed parallel and sequential workloads on scalable parallel machines. In essence this will apply to multiprocessing architectures where a number of CPUs are design to process a number of different processes concurrently (i.e. at the same time). When this happens some processes will have to execute sequentially while others may execute in parallel. The goal of scheduling is to ensure that the multiprocessing is optimal, which is to say that all CPUs are utilized efficiently and that all resources are shared optimally between all the processes that are running. The design of the scheduling system proposed here is based on two principles namely,

1. That parallel programs should be scheduled in a coordinated manner so that they will not severely interfere with each other and the performance for parallel computing becomes predictable. In other words this implies that procedural and data dependence between processes that are executing in parallel is controlled.

2. That parallel programs may time-share resources with sequential programs so that the efficiency of processor utilization can be enhanced and good response to interactive clients can be maintained. This means that the scheduler will schedule both sequential and parallel process in order to improve overall performance.

The paper further discusses the organisation of a registration office through which the two-level scheduling can be realised. In other words, a dedicated agent is designed to monitor the processes that are executing and to use this information to control the scheduling. The essence here is to schedule one parallel process to run with sequential processes. With this approach parallel workloads are scheduled at two different levels. At the first or global level they are co scheduled across the processors, while at the second or local level processes associated with parallel jobs may time-share resources with sequential processes on each processor, which is controlled by a local scheduler. Thus the scheduling scheme is actually a combination of local scheduling and co scheduling.

The basic structure of the two-level scheduling scheme on each processor is depicted in Figure 2.6.

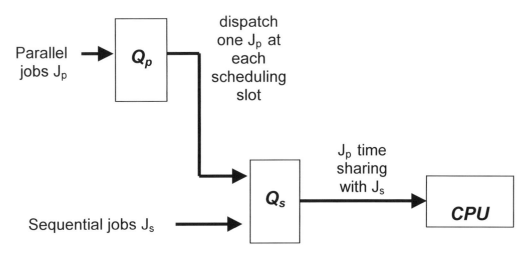

Figure 2.6. Two level scheduling scheme

This arrangement consists of two queues, a queue Q_p at the first level, which is used to coordinate parallel workloads and a sequential queue Q_s at the second level, which is used to coordinate sequential workloads. In this arrangement new sequential processes directly come to the sequential queue and parallel processes will first enter the parallel queue and then be dispatched to the sequential queue before receiving a service. In other words of the two queues only Q_s acts as a dispatcher. Since co scheduling is applied, each time only one parallel process can be dispatched from the parallel queue and thus at any time instant there may only be one parallel process in the sequential queue. If parallel processes associated with the same job are placed at the same place in each parallel queue across the processors and the same scheduling algorithm is applied, they can then be dispatched at the same time. After entering the sequential queue the parallel process on each processor may time-share the service with sequential processes.

The paper further discusses the details of the implementation which provide a very informative read, but the above is offered as an example of some of the issues that need to be considered in the scheduling of parallel processes.

Exercises

2.1   A CPU clock speed is 1GHz; calculate the amount of time it will take the CPU to complete 1000 instructions each using 100 clock cycles.

2.2   Explain the following in relation to process control,
a) Context switch.
b) Thrashing.
c) Multitasking.
d) Multithreading
e) Clustering.

2.3   Explain the 5-state process model and indicate how it is derived from the 3-state process model. Also explain the three levels of scheduling that apply to these states.

2.4   Explain the function of each of the 5 states and the rules governing state transitions.

2.5   Discuss the factors that influence the choice of the time quantum used to trigger the transition of a process from the running state to the ready state.

2.6   Describe the main features of the 6 scheduling policies given in this text.

2.7   Explain how the round robin scheduling guarantees the completion of even the longest jobs. Since each process is allocated a quantum if there are n processes in the queue and a fixed time quantum (Q), calculate what proportion of CPU time is given to each process. For this situation how would you calculate the amount of time that a process has to wait before it is serviced? What is the main disadvantage of this policy?

2.8   Discuss how the following processes would fare in a multi-level feedback scheduling system.

- ·A short CPU-bound process.
- ·A long CPU-bound process.
- ·An I/O Bound process.

2.9   For the processes given in the table below compare the performance of the 6 scheduling policies.

Process	P1	P2	P3	P4	P5
Estimated run-time (T_{ER})	20	11	2	750	1

2.10   Explain the operation of the multi-level feedback queues (MFQ) scheduling system in a single processor computer. Include in your answer a clear description of the scheduling policies that can be used at these levels. Suggest the possible modifications to MFQs that would enhance the performance of the process.

2.11   How do you distinguish between sequential and parallel processes?

2.12   Discuss the problems encountered in scheduling parallel processes.

2.13   Explain the basic principles that distinguish local scheduling from co-scheduling.

2.14   Explain the limitations of the batch scheme for scheduling parallel processes. Suggest a way in which these limitations can be overcome.

2.15   The two level scheduling system of Figure 2.6 aims to provide separate queues for parallel and sequential processes. Explain how this scheme improves the performance of the system.

2.16   The two level scheduling system of Figure 2.6 shows a single CPU to which the jobs are scheduled. Can this scheme work in multiple CPUs? If so, suggest how this can be done.

CHAPTER 3 MEMORY MANAGEMENT

3.1. Introduction

During the time that they are executing all processes reside in the physical memory (RAM) of the computer at the same time. As the processes are running the schedulers decide what to run next, and at the same time the memory management system needs to ensure that the correct process is loaded. Thus, the memory management subsystem is one of the most important parts of the operating system.

Since the early days of computing, there has been a need for more memory than exists physically in a system. Consequently managing the limited physical memory has become one of the most challenging and complex tasks for modern operating systems. This challenge is made more complex by the fact that a multitasking O/S must divide physical memory among the many processes that are running simultaneously, giving each process an appropriate share of memory. Furthermore, the O/S must be able to adjust its behaviour within a wide range of memory sizes, from as little as 16MB to as much as 1GB or more.

Strategies have been developed to overcome this limitation and the most successful of these is virtual memory. Virtual memory makes the system appear to have more memory than it actually has by sharing the available memory between competing processes, as they need it.

3.2. Process loading and swapping

All CPUs operate on the basis of the Fetch-Execute cycle, which means that every instruction is fetched first and then executed. This is done for every instruction in the program until there are no more instructions to execute. In order for the CPU to be able to fetch the instructions quickly, the program has to reside in the main memory. That is to say, program code must be transferred from secondary storage (hard disk) to main memory. This transfer of process code is referred to as process loading (see Figure 3.1). When the program terminates, the code is transferred back (swapped) to the hard disk.

In terms of the 5-state diagram of a process, access to the hard disk for loading and swapping implies that this is an I/O wait.

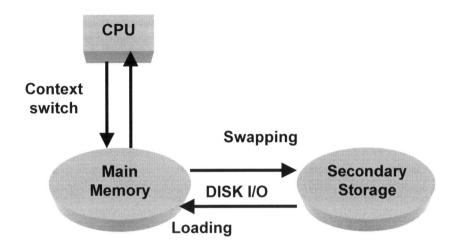

Figure 3.1. Process loading and swapping from secondary storage

All this data transfer between the main memory and the hard disk takes time. The data rates are a feature of the hardware architecture and the type of transfer taking place. Table 3.1 gives an example of transfer rates for some common I/O buses namely the PCI and SCSI adapters for 32-bit and 64-bit buses.

Table 3.1

Bus Type	Clock Frequency	PCI Spec.	Transfer Rate
32 bit	33 MHz	PCI 2.1	132 MB/sec
64 bit	133MHz	PCI X	1066MB/sec
32 bit	33 MHz	SCSI Ultra 2	80 MB/sec
64 bit	66 MHz	SCSI Ultra 4	320 MB/sec

It is seen that the 133MHz PCI X bus can transfer data at 1066MB/sec. Therefore, if the file size is 100Kbytes, the amount of time it takes to transfer can be calculated as follows,

$$T_{TF} = \frac{100 \times 2^{10}}{1066 \times 2^{20}} = \frac{100}{1066 \times 2^{10}} = 91.6 \mu S$$

For the same file size 32 bit, 33 MHz, SCSI Ultra 2 with a rate of 80MB/s will take,

$$T_{TF} = \frac{100 \times 2^{10}}{80 \times 2^{20}} = \frac{100}{80 \times 2^{10}} = 1.2 mS$$

Typically with disk access, besides the actual transfer rates it is necessary to take into account disk related time delays. These include the average seek time (moving the read/write head to the required track) and the average latency (rotation of disk to the required sector). They also need to include controller overhead and queuing delay. Fast hard disks have access times in the region of 10 milliseconds. [10]

By comparison, RAM access times are in the region of 70 nanoseconds. The speed differential between access to RAM and access to HD is given by,

$$S_D = \frac{10 \times 10^{-3}}{70 \times 10^{-9}} = 142857$$

This is useful as a comparison although it has to be said that overall HD performance is significantly influenced by channel speed (transfer rate), interleaving and caching.

For reference purposes, the most common type of RAM at present is the synchronous dynamic RAM (SDRAM). This has a peak transfer rate of around 800MBps. This converts to an equivalent bus frequency of,

$$f_{SDRAM} = \frac{1}{800 \times 2^{20}} = \frac{1.25 \times 10^{-3}}{2^{20}} = 1.192 GHz$$

Newer DDR SDRAM (double-data-rate SDRAM) has a peak transfer rate of 2.1GBps.

3.3.   Memory management subsystem

The memory management subsystem is concerned with ensuring that all the processes that are running have the necessary memory allocated to them. This can be divided into three areas, [13]

1.   Memory management hardware (Memory Management Units (MMUs), RAM, etc.). The MMU is a hardware device responsible for handling memory access by the CPU.

2. Operating system memory management (virtual memory, protection). (Refer to Chapter 2 for Windows kernel memory management features).

3. Application memory management (allocation, de-allocation, garbage collection).

Memory management hardware consists of electronic devices that look after the physical connections and bits transfer. These devices include RAM, MMUs (memory management units), caches, disks, and processor registers.

The memory management component of the operating system controls the way that the hardware works to provide memory resources to programs. The most significant part of this is virtual memory, which creates the illusion that every process has more memory than is actually available. The O/S memory management is also concerned with memory protection and security.

Application memory management refers to the actual process loading and swapping that was mentioned earlier. Most applications or processes that are running have dynamically changing memory requirements. The application memory manager must cope with this while at the same time optimising CPU and memory usage. To summarise therefore, memory management is concerned with providing the following,

1. Enable several processes to appear to execute at the same time (i.e. time share the CPU).

2. Enable processes to share physical memory.

3. Provide satisfactory program execution speeds.

4. Protect one process from another.

3.4. Memory allocation methods

Memory is allocated to processes according to the microprocessor architecture and the way that the memory manager is designed to operate. For example, a memory manager may allocate a fixed size partition to every process. This could be found in embedded micro controller application where the processes that need to run are lightweight and whose size is known. Since only one process can be in memory at any one time, these would typically be single task systems. If multitasking operation is required, such as for example, in real-time systems, then there could be more than one fixed partition in memory. This arrangement was initially used in early IBM360s systems, and it was very useful for two main reasons namely,

1. It allows a number of processes to be stored in memory of different sizes.
2. Memory protection is derived from the fact that the size of partition is known and wrong address generations are easily detected.

Single process system

In embedded computer applications where, it is common for the CPU to run only one process at a time, memory management is simple. The process to be executed is loaded into the free memory space and the rest of the memory space will be unused. Figure 3.2 represents a single process allocation. Such an arrangement is clearly limited in capability and is now found only in simple systems such as games computers. Also early MS-DOS systems operated in this way. While it is still valid to have such a memory model in simple embedded systems, the arrangement is not applicable to multitasking applications.

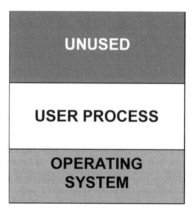

Figure 3.2. Single partition memory with single process allocation.

For multitasking, a necessary extension to this basic model is to permit the loading of more than one process into memory simultaneously, which leads on to alternative schemes considered next.

Fixed partition memory

This scheme follows on from the single partition above, by offering a number of partitions each of which is of a fixed size. Each of these partitions can accommodate a separate process, and therefore multitasking is possible. This memory arrangement is shown in Figure 3.3.

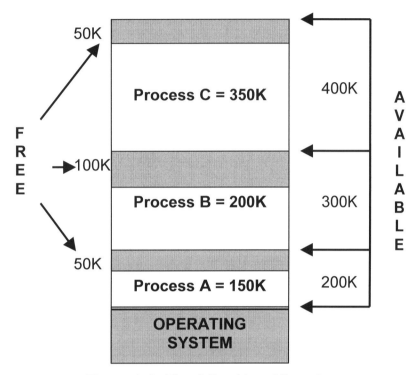

Figure 3.3. Fixed Partition Allocation

In Figure 3.3 the memory is shown consisting of three areas, of size 200K, 300K and 400K respectively, each of which holds a process. If the operating system can support multitasking, all three processes can be active at any one time. In a practical system with this allocation method, the memory manager would control the number and the sizes of partitions. This would in turn depend on the amount of total memory available and the size of processes to be run. Typically, a range of partition sizes would be set up, so that a mixture of large and small processes could be accommodated. Since there is no general way to prevent a process generating an invalid address, memory protection has to be implemented by the operating system and/or hardware. Since the partition sizes are fixed, it is relatively straightforward to implement basic memory protection by using limit registers.

Fixed partition systems are useful in embedded multitasking applications, but they do have limitations. The main problem is in the fact that the fixed size of memory limits the size of the program that can run, and also if a very small program needs to run, then the memory space is under-utilised. Another major concern is internal fragmentation, which is explained next.

Internal fragmentation

During normal operation processes would be loaded into memory and swapped back to secondary storage. As the processes are running, every partition will typically contain unused space, (illustrated by the shaded areas in Figure 3.3) and as a result the total unused space could be considerable. With reference to Figure 3.3 the total combined unused space is 50K+100K+50K=200K.

This type of space distribution is referred to as internal fragmentation because the total available space is fragmented. Internal fragmentation wastes space within partitions, which, if combined would provide sufficient memory to run another process. Another problem with fixed partitions is that large programs cannot fit into all the partitions, and have to wait for a large partition to be freed up.

Variable partition memory

The solution to the fixed partition problems is to allow the partitions to be variable in size at load time. The variable partition method allocates to every process the exact amount of memory that it needs. Initially, processes are loaded into consecutive memory areas as shown in Figure 3.4.

When a process that is in a partition terminates, the occupied space is freed up and this becomes available for the loading of a new process.

After a number of processes have terminated the memory space appears as a series of 'holes' between the active memory areas. Fragmentation is obvious in this case and this can lead to a situation where, even though the total free space is adequate, a new process cannot be started because none of the holes is large enough.

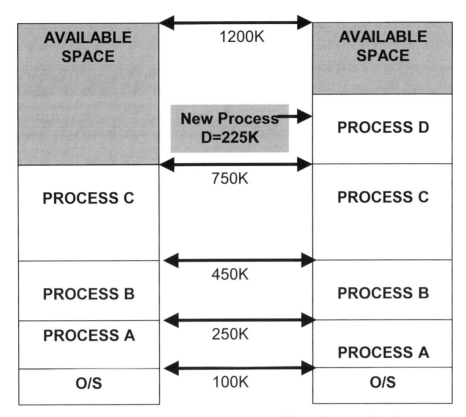

AVAILABLE SPACE	1200K	AVAILABLE SPACE
	New Process D=225K	PROCESS D
PROCESS C	750K	PROCESS C
PROCESS B	450K	PROCESS B
PROCESS A	250K	PROCESS A
O/S	100K	O/S

Figure 3.4. Variable partition allocation method

This situation is illustrated in Figure 3.5 a) in which processes A and C have terminated. The total available space is 150+300+225=675K and yet the largest program that can be accommodated is 300K. Such distribution of the free memory space is called external fragmentation where 'external' refers to space vacated by a process that has terminated. Note that internal fragmentation occurs in the fixed partition scheme where 'internal' implies 'within the space allocated to a process.

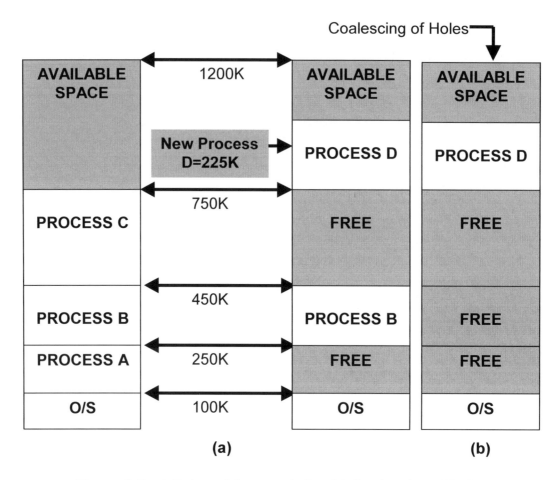

Figure 3.5. a) External fragmentation b) Coalescing of holes

Coalescing of holes

It is frequently the case that a process adjacent to one or more holes will terminate and free its space. The result of this is the creation of two or three adjacent holes. These empty memory locations can then be merged together and utilised as a single hole, as shown in Figure 3.5 b). Here process B has terminated and the holes created by previously running processes A and C are joined up. The combined effect is that the free space is now a contiguous space of 500K. This effect of combining adjacent empty memory locations is referred to as coalescing of holes, and is a significant factor in maintaining fragmentation within usable limits.

It is also possible for the O/S to periodically flush the memory by rearranging the memory allocation to processes in order to eliminate external fragmentation. This is referred to as compaction, and relies on physically moving resident processes in memory to produce the best general fit. The problem with this is that processes have to be suspended while they are being moved. This can produce heavy CPU overheads and therefore it is seldom used. However, when compaction is used, it can either be done at preset intervals, as soon as a process terminates or when a process does not have sufficient memory to load.

3.5.   Storage placement policies

Processes that run in a multitasking system are usually of different sizes and therefore the allocation of memory to every process has to be governed by a placement policy. With the variable partition scheme it is necessary to select the 'best' location to load new processes. Inefficient allocation can delay the loading of a process due to external fragmentation. The following describes a number of such policies have been devised,

- **Best-fit policy-** In this policy when a process arrives, it is placed in a hole where the difference between the hole size and the new process size is the least.

- **First fit policy-** Here the incoming process is placed in the first available hole that can accommodate it.

- **Worst fit policy-** An incoming process is placed in the hole, which leaves the maximum amount of unused space, implying the current largest hole.

These three allocation methods can be illustrated with reference to Figure 3.6. Here, a new process needs to be placed into one of the three available partitions, which are of different sizes. All partitions are large enough to accommodate the process, which is 150K bytes. However each partition will leave a different memory residue. For example,

Using the first fit policy- P1 (150K) fits into 300K leaving 150K free. Partitions 2 and 3 are still free and the three partitions can accommodate any process ranging from 150K-400K. The smallest partition is 150K.

Using the best fit policy- P1 (150K) the least amount of residue is obtained when P1 is placed into 200K leaving 50K FREE Partitions 1 and 3

are still free and the three partitions can now accommodate any process ranging from 50K-400K, where the smallest partition can hold only 50K.

Using the worst fit policy- P1 (150K) the most residue is obtained when P1 is placed into 400K leaving 250K FREE Partitions 1 and 2 are still free and the three partitions can now accommodate any process ranging from 250K-400K, where the smallest partition can hold 250K.

Thus, it is seen that if processes larger than 150K are likely to prevail, then it may well be better to use the worst-fit policy than the best-fit policy. This is because the residue that is left in this case can accommodate larger processes.

Partition 3
400K

New Process A = 150K

Partition 2
200K

Partition 1
300K

Policy	Partition	Residue
Best fit	2	50K
First fit	1	150K
Worst fit	3	250K

OPERATING SYSTEM

Figure 3.6. Placement policies with a table of memory residues

In order to accommodate placement policies and to monitor the size of the memory residue, linked lists are used to describe each partition. Linked lists contain pointers to the size of each hole and its start address.

3.6. Paging

Paging is a very valuable feature of memory management. By dividing memory into equal size pages, processes can be loaded into a number of these pages. Additionally, when a page from one process finishes, a page from another process can easily replace it because all the pages are of the same size. Therefore, paged memory divides all memory in equal size pages, each with a page number and a displacement contained in the 'Page Table'. Process pages do not need to be contiguous since allocation is done on a page-by-page basis. Furthermore, it is possible to relocate processes by only changing the reference in the page table.

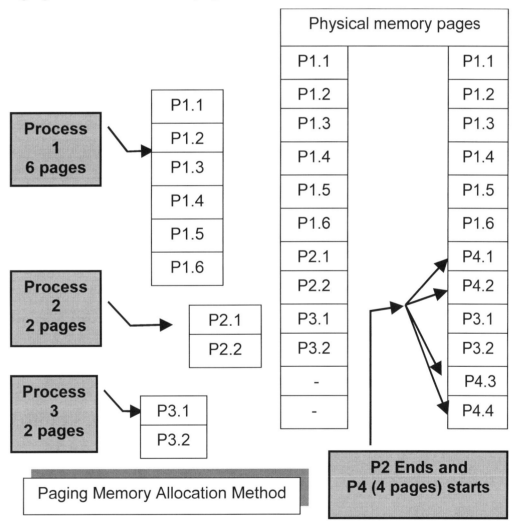

Figure 3.7. Paged memory system

With reference to Figure 3.7, when the processes P1, P2 and P3 are first loaded, the memory pages are filled in a sequential manner. As the processes run, and pages terminate, some pages leave physical memory. Figure 3.7 suggests that P2 finishes and vacates two pages that it occupied. Another process P4, which is four pages long, subsequently enters, and occupies the four pages that are free. It is seen that when P4 enters, it occupies pages that are not contiguous. This is perfectly acceptable because process pages do not need to be contiguous since allocation is done on a page-by-page basis. A paging table takes care of locating pages for every process and keeping track of where pages are.

Implementation of paging

Paging is a particularly useful in a multitasking environment with virtual memory. Allocating the pages of memory to processes is a very complex task if the overall performance needs to be optimised. Splitting a process into a number of pages means that when the process runs the paging system needs to monitor and schedule multiple parts of each process. The solution to this problem lies in the way a specific memory location is addressed in a paging environment.

A page address is made up of two components a page number *(p)* and a displacement *(d)* within that page that identifies a particular memory location. In this manner, and in the knowledge that all pages are of the same size, it is relatively easy to locate a desired physical address using the equation,

$$P_{address} = p \times size \times + d \qquad (3.2)$$

For example, assume that all pages are 4K and that we want to find the location of a byte in memory with page *p=4* and offset *d=32*. According to equation 3.2, that location is given as follows

$$P_{address} = 4 \times (4 \times 2^{10}) + 32 = 16,416$$

The form *(p, d)* used to locate a physical memory location is easy to represent using binary notation. For example if the page size is 2K then the displacement value is made up of 11 bits. (i.e.2^{11}=2K). If a 16-bit address bus is used, this means that 5 bits remain for the representation of the page number. In other words, there are 2^5=32 page numbers. Figure 3.8 shows an example of how a 16 bit address can be divided into the p and d fields. Here, the page number uses the high 5 bits and therefore has a value range of 0 to 31 or 32 pages. The displacement value uses 11 bits and therefore has a range of 0 to 2023. This means a system based on this scheme would have 32 pages each with 2024 locations. Increasing the page size to 4K would reduce the number of pages to 16, since the total address space is still 16–bits.

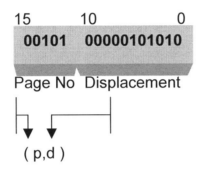

Figure 3.8. 16 bit address example

Consider an example, using a 16-bit address 0010100000101010. This can be divided into page and displacement values,

	Page	Displacement
Binary	00101	00000101010
Decimal	5	42

Hence this location can be expressed as the paging address of (5, 42).

Example

A computer uses an 20 bit address system, with 6 bits used as a page address and 14 bits used as a displacement. Given that a paging address is 00111100000011100010, calculate the total number of pages, page size, paging address, and the location of the page in physical memory.

Solution-

Number of pages (6 bits) = 2^6=64 pages

Page size (max. discplacement)= 2^{14}= 16K

Paging address: Page number (6 bits)   001111= 15 decimal

Displacement (14 bits)   00000011100010= 226 decimal

Hence the paging address of (15,226).

Physical location: page number x page size + displacement

= 15x16K+226=245986

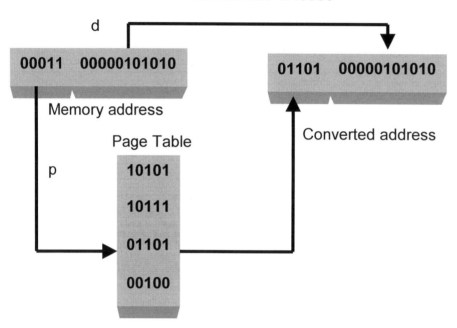

Figure 3.9. Relocation using page table

As mentioned earlier, page relocation can be done by only changing an entry in the page table. This is shown in Figure 3.9 where the converted address on the right is made up of the 5-bit page number and in this case an 11-bit displacement. The displacement remains the same, but the page number changes according to the pointer p in the page table. If for example, p changed to 0010, then location 2, i.e. (10111) in the page table would be used to reference the page.

3.7. Simple segmentation

Segmentation is the principle of dividing memory into segments. Segments are larger than pages and the main reason for them is to provide additional control over the addressing and the allocation of memory. Segments can be configured to be variable in length, or as in the case of the Intel 8086 microprocessor, all segments are the same length of 64K. Figure 3.10 can be used to explain the principle of simple segmentation. Here, two separate processes are loaded into memory. They are dispersed in the main memory into segments that are of different sizes. The reason for this is that different processes are themselves of a different size, and segments are allocated to reflect this. Once again, as in paging, segments belonging to a process do not need to be contiguous because the location of every segment is stored in a segment table.

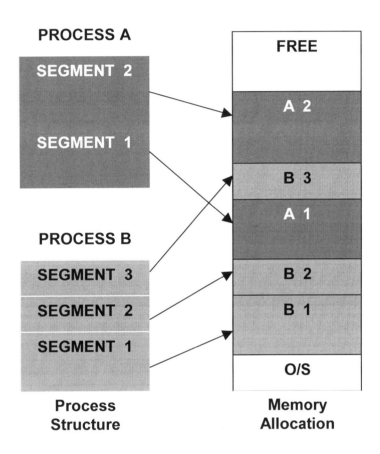

Figure 3.10. Simple segmentation

Segment addressing

The conversion of a logical address into a segment address is similar to the paging system in so far as two parameters are used to locate a memory address. Namely, the segment reference s, and the displacement d, within that segment are used to locate an address.

A process segment table, such as that shown in Figure 3.11 contains the size and the base address of each segment.

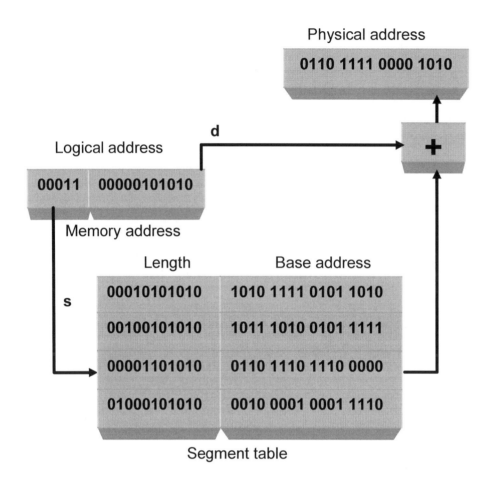

Figure 3.11. Addressing using a segment table

The logical address contains a reference to the segment and the offset address. The physical address is obtained by locating the base address of the segment and adding to this the displacement. Thus, for example a logical address given in Figure 3.11 is made up of the LHS five bits that point to the segment. The other bits contain the offset. The segment pointer s, points to the segment with the base address of 0110 1110 1110 0000. The physical address of the memory location is obtained by adding this base address to the displacement. This is shown in Table 3.2.

Table 3.2

Logical address	0	0	0	1	1	0	0	0	0	0	1	0	1	0	1	0
Base address	0	1	1	0	1	1	1	0	1	1	1	0	1	0	1	0
Physical address	0	1	1	0	1	1	1	1	0	0	0	0	1	0	1	0

Therefore in general, a segmented address reference requires the following steps,

- Separate the segment number and the displacement from the logical address.
- Use the segment number to index the segment table and obtain the segment base address and length.
- Check that the offset does not exceed segment length; if it does then an invalid address error is generated.
- Calculate the required physical address by adding offset to the base address.

In a shared-memory environment segmentation can be used to protect one process from another. Since the CPU is not able to distinguish between instructions and simply executes the bytes that have been fetched, if there is a memory error, and the instruction that has been fetched is not the correct one, the program will fail. Thus, it is necessary to protect memory space allocated to a program during execution. Segmentation provides the size of the segment that is being referenced; it can use this to check for any addressing errors.

For example, on the Intel x86 architecture, the Global Descriptor Table (GDT) and Local Descriptor Tables (LDT) are used to reference segments in the computer's memory. Together these are used to protect memory by performing checks on address limits, privilege levels etc. Every memory reference is checked before the memory cycle begins and any violation results in an exception. Detailed explanation of the Intel memory management system can be found in Intel literature. [14]

3.8. Cache memory

Cache memory is RAM that is used to store recently used information so that it may be retrieved faster. The idea behind this is that recently used data will be needed again soon and this is referred to as the principle of temporal locality. Cache memory exists in conjunction with main memory and focuses on the contents of main memory, from which it will take data. When data is first loaded into RAM the source is generally through an I/O subsystem, which is relatively slow. Once it is inside RAM and being used, there comes a point where it has to be discarded from RAM. If this data is needed again in the near future, it has to be retrieved from its original source. Cache memory enables storage of this data in separate RAM, which makes it possible to access this data more quickly. It should be quite obvious that an entry in the cache must be indexed to the original data in the RAM. This is so that it can be retrieved in the correct way.

When a process requires access to data it first checks the cache. If the data is found in the cache then it is used and this is referred to as a cache hit. The percentage of accesses that result in cache hits is known as the hit rate or hit ratio of the cache. The alternative to a hit is a cache miss, where data is not found in the cache and has to be retrieved from source (i.e. hard disk). In this case the retrieved data is kept in the cache for possible future use. Typically a cache will have limited space and it is not possible to store in it all the data that is used in the execution of processes. There comes a point where cache entries have to be deleted in order that new entries may be entered. This is usually done using the least recently used (LRU) policy, which replaces the cache items that were not used recently. This agrees with the general principle of temporal locality identified earlier.

Cache write policy

As mentioned earlier RAM is used to read from as well as to write data. When data is written to the cache at some point it must be stored in secondary storage and this is referred to as the cache write policy. There are three basic types of write back policy as follows,

Write through: In this policy every write to the cache also includes a write to the secondary store. Thus every cache write is mirrored to the secondary storage. This provides very good data consistency but is slower because of multiple write operations.

Write back: In this policy not every write to the cache is replicated to the secondary storage. Instead the secondary storage is updated only when the data has been evicted from the cache. In other words, while data is in the cache it is permitted to change and each of the changes is being tracked. Modified cache data is marked as dirty, and when it is evicted from the cache it is written to secondary storage. This policy is faster than write through and offers a good level of data integrity.

No-write allocation: There is no write back in this policy and only the processor reads are cached. This is the fastest of the three but it provides no data integrity.

Each of the above policies has its applications and although some are faster than others the issue of data consistency with these can be of concern. However writing to secondary storage does not only happen from the cache. As a result the values stored in the cache may become out of date (stale). To maintain data consistency caches use coherency protocols.

3.9. Cache applications

Cache is used whenever devices or applications require memory intensive activity, where cache memory speeds enhance the overall operation. This happens with CPUs, hard drives and other I/O devices as well as networking applications that work with large databases (i.e. DNS databases use cache to store recent IP addresses and domain names). Each of these cache applications is different both in storage capacity and configuration.

CPU cache: CPU activity involves the manipulation of data used in processing and small cache memories relatively close to the CPU can be made to work faster than conventional RAM. It is common to have a number of these small cache memories near the CPU each dedicated to different CPU activity. CPU caches are typically managed entirely by hardware and they connect to the CPU via a high speed bus.

Disk cache: These caches are dedicated to storing disk I/O data. They can be implemented separately or be a part of main memory. For example the page cache is stored in main memory and it is used to store recently used process pages. This configuration requires that the cache is managed by the operating system, since it is physically located in main memory.

Other cache applications: In networked environments a large amount of data is transferred and frequently the data that has been transferred will be required soon. To avoid transferring the same data, caches are used to store the data and reuse it as necessary. For example, a web browser manages a cache of recently visited web pages. In larger networks, dedicated servers are used to provide proxy cache services to serve the web page requests for the network.

The domain naming service (DNS) in networked environments ensures that all domain names are mapped to the appropriate IP addresses. DNS servers are networked to communicate IP information and typically this is contained in large data tables that contain the data. To speed access a DNS daemon caches recently used domain names maps to their IP addresses. IP allocation on the Internet is in the main dynamic and many changes are to be expected during normal operation. It is therefore common to use read only or write-though caches in order to reduce complexity of the coherency protocols.

Caching is also very common in all large databases where searching query results and indexing and data dictionary information is stored in a cache. This applies to large database applications such as Oracle as well as Internet search engines and e-commerce applications.

It can be seen that the term cache has a variety of specific applications; however in all cases the main purpose of the cache is to reduce accesses to the underlying slower storage. The main performance gain occurs because there is a good chance that the same datum will be read from cache multiple times, or that written data will soon be read. [17]

Exercises

3.1   Explain what is meant by the following terms in memory management: coalescing of holes, internal and external fragmentation, and compaction.

3.2   Given that the 133MHz PCI X bus can transfer data at 1066MB/sec. Calculate the amount of time to transfer 100Kbytes.

3.3   For the same file size calculate the transfer time on a 32 bit, 33 MHz, SCSI Ultra 2 with a rate of 80MB/s.

3.4 Explain how paging is used to arrange process memory. What are the advantages over other storage policies?

3.5 Why is segmentation used in memory management and what are its advantages? Provide examples.

3.6 Explain how a logical address consisting of 18 bits could be converted to a paging address where each page was 1K. How many pages would be available?

3.7 In a segmented memory system an address of 24 bits is used to support up to 256 segments. Describe this system and how it could be implemented. What would be the maximum size of each segment?

3.8 For a Pentium processor with 32-bit addressing the maximum addressable space is 4Gigabytes (4.3x109). If size=4K. How many virtual pages can be addressed? If each table entry is 5 bytes how much memory space is required for the whole table?

3.9 A computer uses an 18-bit address system with 6 bits used as a page address and 12 bits used as a displacement. Calculate the page size, the total number of pages and express the following address as a paging address; 001110000000111000.

3.10 In a paged-segmented system, a virtual address consists of 32 bits of which 12 are a displacement, 11 bits are a segment number and 9 bits are a page number. Calculate: page size, maximum segment size, maximum number of pages, and maximum number of segments.

3.11 Explain why cache memory is based on the principle of temporal locality.

3.12 How is cache used in a typical application? Provide examples.

3.13 How do you define a cache miss? What affects on performance does a cache miss have as opposed to a cache hit?

3.14 Describe the essential features of the 3 main cache write policies, their advantages and disadvantages.

3.15 Discuss the various cache applications, including CPU cache, disk cache and other cache applications.

CHAPTER 4 BUS ARCHITECTURE

4.1. Introduction

Buses are used in computer architectures to carry signals between devices. A parallel bus consists of a number of conductors arranged in parallel and each of these will carry the signals of one bit. An 8-bit bus will have eight of these conductors running in parallel and so with the 16-bit, 32-bit, 64-bit etc. Inside a CPU chip for example, these buses are made of a highly conductive metal such as gold (Au) and they link the internal components of a CPU. Serial buses tend to be used to connect peripheral devices, which are typically much slower than the internal components of a CPU. With serial buses, the data bits are transmitted in a series of pulses and the transmitting and receiving ends are configured to understand the signals by using a serial protocol. All communications protocols define the signals that are used in order that devices can communicate effectively and in all cases the sending and receiving devices must support the same protocol. Typically bus specifications include the electrical signal definitions as well as the protocols that are used for communications.

Buses can be parallel buses, which carry data words in parallel on multiple wires, or serial buses, which carry data in bit-serial form. The addition of extra power and control connections, differential drivers, and data connections in each direction usually means that most serial buses have more conductors than the minimum of one used in the 1-Wire and UNI/O serial buses. As data rates increase, the problems of timing skew, power consumption, electromagnetic interference and crosstalk across parallel buses become more and more pronounced. Consequently a serial bus can be operated at higher overall data rates than a parallel bus, despite having fewer electrical connections. This is because a serial bus has no timing skew or crosstalk. USB, FireWire, and Serial ATA are examples of this. [21]

Most computers have both internal and external buses. An internal bus connects all the internal components of a computer to the motherboard (and thus, the CPU and internal memory). These types of buses are also referred to as a local bus, because they are intended to connect to local devices, not to those in other machines or external to the computer. An external bus connects external peripherals to the motherboard.

Buses are designed to run at different speeds because communication between different devices in the computer architecture cannot support the same data transfer rates. This is because devices perform different functions and each of these has time limitations. For example loading data from physical RAM into a CPU register can happen much faster than moving data from the hard disk to physical RAM. The reason for this is that hard disks include mechanical devices, which rotate the disk and align the disk heads with the correct disk sector etc. This mechanical action constrains the speeds of data transfer between the disk and the CPU. This is just one example, but there are many other examples where physical device limitations constrain the speed of transfer of data.

4.2. Computer Buses

As already mentioned in Chapter 1 buses are essentially a group of conductors, which carry electrical signals between components. The CPU itself, as a chip will have an internal architecture that will include buses. Outside the CPU, devices on the motherboard connected to the CPU will also have buses that interconnect them. Thus it is seen that buses can be implemented at different hardware levels.

In a very simplified sense however the CPU controls all the activity of a computer system. Much of this activity concerns the movement of data. For example, instructions and data travel back and forth from the CPU to memory over the data bus while I/O ports enable communications with the outside world. Before the CPU can access memory, register or an I/O device, the address of this component needs to be known. Therefore, the address bus is used to identify the source and destination addresses of components participating in a connection. Once a connection is established between components the control bus is needed to tell these components what to do.

Address bus - Address bus is a collection of conductors connecting the CPU with main memory and I/O space and it is used to identify particular address locations within the memory or I/O space. Looking at the motherboard printed circuit board, the bus is seen as thin copper strips running in parallel between components. The width of the address bus determines the number of unique location that can be addressed, for example,

- 8 bit => 2^8 = 256 addresses.
- 16 bit => 2^{16} = 64k addresses.
- 32 bit => 2^{32} = 4G addresses.

Data Bus - Data bus is used to transmit data from one part of a computer to another. It can be visualised as a highway on which data travels within a computer. The address bus locates the source and destination addresses, and the data bus carries the data.

Control bus - Control bus enables correct exchange of information between components. The control bus carries information such as READ, WRITE, RESET etc between the CPU and other devices within the computer. While the data bus carries actual data being processed and the address bus carries the location of this data, the control bus carries signals that report the status of the various devices.

Bus cycles

As the microprocessor program executes, data is transferred to and from memory and I/O devices. Each instance of data transfer from one part of the system to another is called a bus cycle. The timing of these cycles is done by the CPU clock signal. As the program executes, the information that is communicated over the bus can be an instruction fetch, memory read, memory write, read from an input or write to an output port. The length of time taken to perform these is timed in the number of clock cycles. The duration of the unit clock cycle is determined by the CPU clock speed, which determines how fast an instruction can be performed. For example, as shown earlier a frequency of 1GHz gives a clock cycle of 1nS.

All instructions that are executing have some reference to the CPU clock. Synchronous communications imply that all activity is synchronised with the CPU clock, and for each stage of the communications a number of complete clock cycles are allocated. In this type of arrangement the time taken to complete the communication or instruction can be calculated very precisely. Asynchronous communication occurs at unpredictable times, and at random frequency. An example is an interrupt that stops current execution of a program and then an interrupt service routine (ISR) is executed. However it is important to note that even though communication is not synchronous, all events occur at integer values of clock cycles. This is to say, it is not possible for an event to be recognised if it occurs in the middle of a clock cycle. Thus all communication relates to the unit bus cycle of the particular CPU architecture.

Typically, at the beginning of a bus cycle the CPU issues a code to the address bus to locate memory or I/O device to be accessed. Next, the CPU issues an activity command on the control bus. Third the CPU either receives or transmits data over the data bus. The CPU keeps track of the instruction sequence using the instruction pointer register, which contains the address of the next instruction to be executed. The programme that is currently running determines this instruction and the CPU then proceeds with executing all the instructions sequentially until the programme terminates. (See Chapter 5 of this text).

Input – Output communications

A major requirement of all computer systems is to communicate with other computers and peripheral devices. Therefore a brief description of some of the input/output standards and systems is considered next.

I/O bus

This bus is used to facilitate communication between the CPU and the I/O peripheral device. Peripheral device speeds are considerably slower than CPU speeds and the I/O bus takes care of synchronisation during communication. This avoids data corruption. There are a variety of I/O buses available, for example, Industry Standard Architecture (ISA) has a 16 bit parallel data flow and was a standard for many years although it has now been virtually phased out. Peripheral Component Interconnect (PCI) bus and the expanded PCI-e are now the standard used in PCs. (More details will be given later in this text).

Bus characteristics

In order to connect devices buses need to be designed and configured to carry the required signals. Figure 4.1 shows the information that a bus would typically include. From Figure 4.1 it is seen that buses must contain the address, data and control signals. Address bus tells the devices where to locate each other, data is the information that is transferred between them, and the control signals include information on how the device will respond. For example, assume that you have to read the value of data, which is stored in memory location FF0Ah. The address location FF0A is placed on the address bus as a 16-bit binary value which points to a location in memory containing the corresponding data. Having been located, this data are placed on the data bus and the READ signal is placed on the control bus to indicate to the CPU that a READ cycle should be performed.

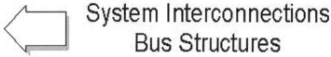 System Interconnections
Bus Structures

- Bus - Set of signals connecting two or more devices
  Address + Data + Control signals

- Used to interconnect CPU - Memory - I/O devices

- Bus characteristics - standards
  Signals / Pin connections / Voltage levels /
  Signal timing / Connectors ..

Figure 4.1. Computer bus characteristics

Clearly all this activity cannot happen at the same time and therefore a timing waveform is produced to show the sequence of timed events that are needed to achieve this. Figure 4.2 shows the basic timing waveform for a PCI bus, during a simple memory, READ operation as described earlier.

PCI Bus - Read Transaction

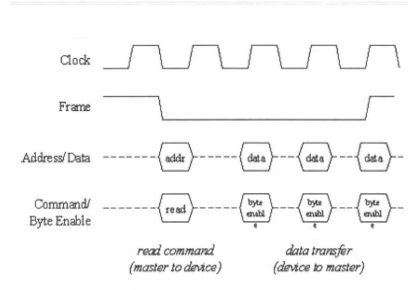

Figure 4.2. PCI bus timing waveform (basic form)

It is seen here that the timing waveforms are synchronised with the system clock. Which is to say that all signals change state at the points of clock transitions and do so in a prescribed sequence. Thus from Figure 4.2 it is seen that a control signal called FRAME is used to signal the start of the operation. At the low level transition the FRAME signal enables the bus and the address value (in binary) is loaded onto the address bus. In order to conserve space, the address and data buses are multiplexed in time while the control signals Command/Byte Enable determine whether the bus is used as an address or data bus (respectively). This is seen in Figure 4.2, where as soon as the FRAME signal goes low, the command shows that a READ cycle is active and this means that at this point in the communication the bus contains an address value. During the next clock cycle, the READ has been completed and the Byte enable signal indicates that DATA is available on the bus. This is only a simple example and a more detailed description of the PCI bus will be covered later on in this chapter. The important aspect is to appreciate at this point is that all action needs to be sequenced correctly in order to enable accurate communication between devices.

4.3. Buses hierarchy

Modern computer architectures contain a large number of components and all of these contribute to the overall operation of the system. Since these components operate at different speeds the buses that interconnect them are different. Figure 4.3 shows the basic arrangements of buses in a typical modern computer system. From this figure it is seen that the system bus connects the CPU and main memory. The expansion bus is slower and all the interfaces are connected to this bus. In order to synchronise between the expansion bus and the system bus a dedicated bus interface unit controller is provided.

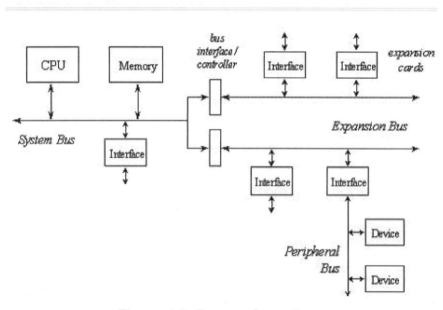

Figure 4.3. Bus configurations

4.4. The Dual Independent Bus (DIB) architecture

This bus was first implemented in the Pentium Pro processor and it was created to enhance the bandwidth of the processor bus. Having two (dual) independent buses enables the Pentium II processor to access data from either of its two buses simultaneously and in parallel, rather than in a sequential manner as in a single bus system. The processor reads and writes data to and from the Level 2 cache using a specialised high-speed bus called the backside bus. This bus is separate from the system bus, which connects the CPU to main memory (called the frontside bus). The DIB architecture allows the processor to use both buses simultaneously, and consequently provides enhanced performance. Together the Dual Independent Bus architecture improvements provide up to three times the bandwidth performance of a single bus architecture processor - as well as supporting the evolution to a 100MHz system bus. [16] A typical present-day desktop computer system with a single processor arrangement of buses is shown in Figure 4.4.

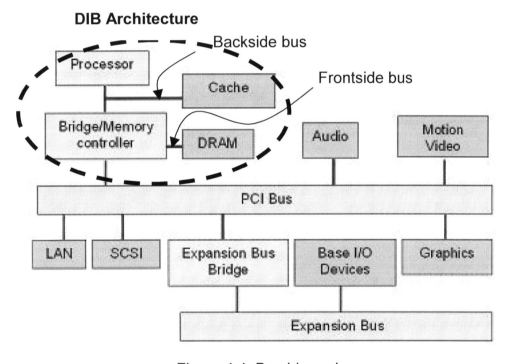

Figure 4.4. Bus hierarchy

Here the CPU links to the system Cache memory via a dedicated bus (backside bus). A bridge/memory controller connects this to the main memory via another bus (the frontside bus) and also connects to the peripheral buses. Each of these buses operates at different speeds and the controller maintains synchronisation between them. The bridge acts as data buffer so that the speeds of PCI may differ from the processor I/O capability.

In a multiprocessor configuration bridges to the system bus may connect one or more PCI buses. The system bus supports only the processor/cache units, main memory and the PCI bridges. The use of bridges keeps the PCI independent of the processor speed yet provides the ability to transfer data rapidly. This is shown in Figure 4.5 where a number of CPUs with internal caches are connected to a common system bus. This bus in turn connects to the main memory and peripheral devices via different buses. A number of bridges provide the connections to the different peripheral devices.

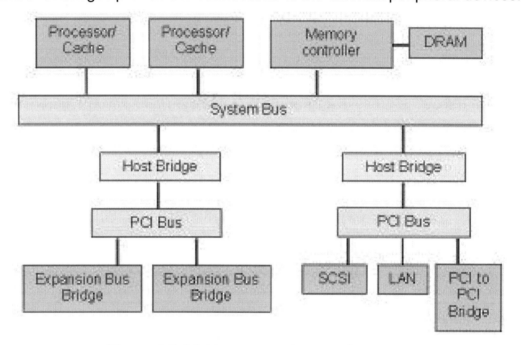

Figure 4.5. Multiprocessor bus configuration

The system bus is the main bus that connects the CPU to main physical memory (RAM). It is fast enough to support the physical RAM devices and these are typically slower than the CPU register devices. Figure 4.6 shows the typical characteristics of the system bus where it is seen that it operates at frequencies of up to 100MHz.

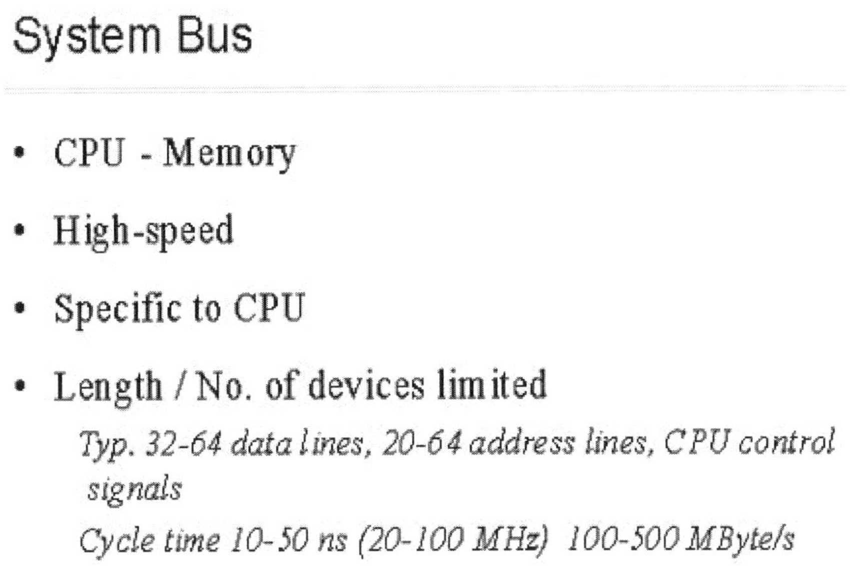

System Bus

- CPU - Memory
- High-speed
- Specific to CPU
- Length / No. of devices limited
  Typ. 32-64 data lines, 20-64 address lines, CPU control signals
  Cycle time 10-50 ns (20-100 MHz) 100-500 MByte/s

Figure 4.6. System bus

With CPUs that contain internal cache memory the system bus is referred to as the front-side bus, and the bus that connects the CPU with the cache is referred to as the backside bus. The backside bus is faster and functions at frequencies around 200MHz. Table 4.1 shows a brief summary of buses used in the Intel Pentium architecture. [17]

Table 4.1 Intel architecture internal bus details

Intel	Pentium Processor version	II	III	IV
CPU Speed		233-450 MHz -	450-1K MHz -	1.4-2.2 GHz
L2 Cache	L2 cache memory, also called the *secondary cache*, resides on a separate chip from the microprocessor chip. Although, more and more microprocessors are including L2 caches into their architectures. Access to CPU via Backside Bus	512 KB, half speed	256 KB, full speed	256 KB, full speed
Front-Side Bus Speed	The bus within a microprocessor that connects the CPU with main memory. It's used to communicate between the motherboard and other components in a computer system.	100 MHz	133 MHz	400 MHz

Expansion bus

The expansion bus connects the CPU to external devices and typically the speed is not a critical issue because usually these devices cannot respond in time even if they receive data at high speeds. Figure 4.7 shows the typical characteristics of the expansion bus and two common buses are identified. The Industry Standard Architecture (ISA) bus has been used for a long time and it runs at 8MHz. This bus is largely outdated and the PCI bus is de-facto standard in most modern PCs. The Peripheral Components Interface bus (PCI) is much faster and is widely used in modern PCs. Other expansion buses include Multibus, futurebus, VME Bus etc.

Multibus was specifically designed for use in industrial systems. This was necessary because industrial applications require a robust and consistent standard with expansion capabilities that can support the design of complex industrial systems. It was developed by Intel Corporation and adopted as the IEEE 796 bus. [18]

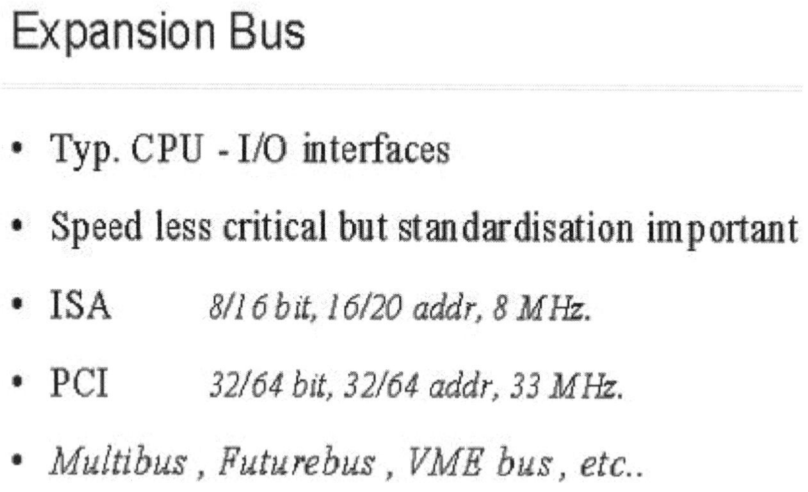

Expansion Bus

- Typ. CPU - I/O interfaces
- Speed less critical but standardisation important
- ISA   *8/16 bit, 16/20 addr, 8 MHz.*
- PCI   *32/64 bit, 32/64 addr, 33 MHz.*
- *Multibus , Futurebus , VME bus , etc..*

Figure 4.7. Expansion bus

Peripheral bus

As the name implies the peripheral bus describes the connection between the main system bus and peripheral devices. A large number of peripheral devices continue to be developed daily and standard bus interfaces enable these to be connected to computer equipment from different manufacturers. This in turn means that different standards are used for different applications. For example, the Universal Serial Bus (USB) is used for interfacing peripheral devices to standard computer equipment. On the other hand controller area network (CAN) bus is designed for use in automotive and process control equipment. Figure 4.8 shows the basic characteristics of a peripheral bus. Here the diagram depicts a daisy chain which means that each device that is connected to the bus links to the next one in the chain, unless it is the last device to connect in which case it requires a terminator resistor to absorb the signal so that it does not bounce on the bus. For example, the IEEE-488 allows up to 15 devices to share a single eight-bit parallel electrical bus by daisy chaining connections. The IEEE-488 is a short-range, digital communications bus specification that has been in use for over 30 years. Originally created for use with automated test equipment, the standard is still in wide use for that purpose. IEEE-488 is also commonly known as HP-IB (Hewlett-Packard Interface Bus) and GPIB (General Purpose Interface Bus).

Peripheral Bus

- Computer - Peripheral devices

- Standardisation important for multi-vendor systems

- IEEE-488 , IDE , CAN , USB ...

- SCSI -

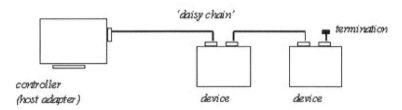

Figure 4.8. Peripheral bus

4.5.   Input-output buses

Universal Serial Bus (USB)

USB was introduced in 1998 as a new standard for connecting external peripherals to a PC without the use of expansion cards. It allows up to 127 devices to be connected through one port at speeds of up to 480Mbit/S (USB 2.0 – high speed). A standard serial port in comparison can receive data from only one device at a time at rates of up to 115Kbits/S. At present USB has become the de facto industry standard for modern peripheral communications. USB 2.0 is suitable for high-performance devices such as high-quality video conferencing cameras, high-resolution scanners, and high-density storage devices.

Firewire

Also known as IEEE-1394, i.Link, is a high-speed serial interface that was originally developed by Apple, who called it FireWire; this name became popular, but Apple owns the rights to it, and many companies refused to pay to license the name. The IEEE-1394 is licence free and therefore is often used to refer to this standard. It is a serial interface that supports,

- Dozens of daisy-chained devices.
- Speeds of up to 400 Mbits/S.
- Hot swapping, and plug-and-play.

Small Computer System Interface SCSI

SCSI is a parallel interface standard used to connect peripheral devices to computers. Compared to standard serial and parallel ports, SCSI provides faster data transmission rates (up to 80 megabytes per second). Additionally, many devices can be attached to a single SCSI port and the SCSI controller provides this. As a result SCSI is very popular with server computers that use RAID arrays i.e. redundant arrays of inexpensive disks). Some features of the SCSI standard are briefly outlined next. [19]

SCSI devices are connected in a daisy chain as shown in Figure 4.9. A SCSI chain (all of devices on a controller) must have a terminator at both ends so that the signals do not bounce back onto the bus. This terminator is typically a resistor, which absorbs the signal when it reaches the termination point.

- SCSI -

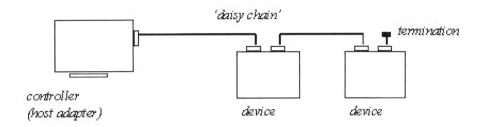

Figure 4.9. Daisy chain

SCSI Versions

SCSI comes in three varieties: SCSI 1, SCSI 2, and SCSI 3.

- **SCSI 1** supports up to 8 devices, with speeds of 5-MBps. One of the devices is required to be the controller card (so you can add 7 additional devices to the controller).

- **SCSI 2** (also known as Ultra-2), which is more popular than SCSI 1, supports up to 16 devices (one of which has to be the adapter card or controller) and supports a higher transfer speed. Ultra 2 SCSI currently allows transfer speeds of up to 80 MBytes/sec over a 16-bit bus.

- **SCSI 3** is sometimes referred to as Ultra-3 SCSI. Ultra-3 SCSI increases the throughput rate of the interface from 80 Mbps to 160 Mbps. The new standard for this transfer rate is referred to as Ultra160/M.

These higher speeds available in Ultra SCSI are due, in large part, to improvements in the processing speeds of the controller's chips.

SCSI limitations

Increasing transfer speed introduces problems to do with the integrity of data transfer. This problem occurs when the receiver cannot keep up with the transmitter and as a result data is lost and communication has to be repeated. In order to minimise this the length of a SCSI cable must not be longer than 1.5 meters. However if communication fails for any reason, the transmission has to be repeated and this is done by retries.

Retries

If a device is attempting to communicate over a channel, but the receiver at the other end signals back that the data was corrupt, the sender then "retries" the transmission. In general retries consume time and processing and if too many of these occur, the speed benefits of the bus become insignificant. Namely,

- Constant retries due to bad connection will significantly reduce the actual data throughput.
- In large RAID arrays the price of retries can affect real-time performance. For example the performance of large server arrays, RAID arrays and video-on-demand systems would not be functional in systems that have a large number of retries. For this reason the number of drives connected should be limited. (i.e. it is not prudent to install 15 drives into a single tower).

In order to address issue relating to retries, a type of SCSI bus called "Low Voltage Differential" or LVD has been introduced. [20] In LVD SCSI systems, two data lines are provided. One sends the signals in the correct polarity and the other (differential bus) provides a second set of data lines being driven with the opposite electrical polarity. For example, if +5 volts in the standard data line represent a "one" bit, that same "one" bit is echoed on the differential data line as -5 volts. In this manner, there is a higher overall voltage swing to represent the data, which makes it easier to detect. Because the two lines contain the same signal (reflected), any noise that might enter the lines will be cancelled out at the receiving end. As a result LVD SCSI can transmit signals over cable lengths of up to 25 meters. Since the SCSI protocols remain unaltered, LVD is fully compatible with the existing single-ended SCSI components. The only requirement is for devices to identify whether LVD is supported and a dedicated on-board circuit determines which type of SCSI bus the device is using, and configures the drive operation to the appropriate bus capability. Thus, LVD devices will work on SCSI-1and SCSI-2 bus segments. Older SCSI-1 and SCSI-2 single-ended devices will work on an LVD bus.

Another feature supported by the new generation of Adaptec Ultra160 LVD host adapters is both CRC (Cyclic Redundancy Checking) and Domain Validation, which scan the system for proper configuration. However, these adapters limit cable length to 12 meters. Some characteristics of SCSI are summarised in Table 4.2

Table 4.2 SCSI characteristics according to version

SCSI Type	Max Cable Length (meters)	Max Speed (MBps)	Max Number of Devices
SCSI-1	6	5	8
SCSI-2	6	5-10	8 or 16
Fast SCSI-2	3	10-20	8
Wide SCSI-2	3	20	16
Fast Wide SCSI-2	3	20	16
Ultra SCSI-3, 8-bit	1.5	20	8
Ultra SCSI-3, 16-bit	1.5	40	16
Ultra-2 SCSI	12	40	8
Wide Ultra-2 SCSI	12	80	16
Ultra-3 (Ultra160/m) SCSI	12	160	16

A large amount of literature is available on the various buses that are in current use. Table 4.3 provides a summary of the internal buses and these are classified as being either parallel or serial. [21]

Table 4.3 Examples of internal computer buses

INTERNAL BUSES Parallel	Serial
ASUS Media Bus proprietary, used on some ASUS Socket 7 motherboards	1-Wire:
CAMAC for instrumentation systems	HyperTransport:
Extended ISA or EISA	I²C
Industry Standard Architecture or ISA	PCI Express or PCIe
Q-Bus, a proprietary bus developed by Digital Equipment Corporation for their PDP and later VAX computers.	Serial Peripheral Interface Bus or SPI bus
MicroChannel or MCA	FireWire i.Link or IEEE 1394
MBus	
Multibus for industrial systems	
NuBus or IEEE 1196	
OPTi local bus used on early Intel 80486 motherboards.	
Peripheral Component Interconnect or PCI	
S-100 bus or IEEE 696, used in the Altair and similar microcomputers	
SBus or IEEE 1496	
VESA Local Bus or VLB or VL-bus	
VMEbus, the VERSAmodule Eurocard bus	
STD Bus for 8- and 16-bit microprocessor systems	
Unibus, a proprietary bus developed by Digital Equipment Corporation for their PDP-11 and early VAX computers.	

Table 4.4 provides a summary of the external buses and these are classified as being either parallel or serial.

Table 4.4 Examples of external computer buses

EXTERNAL Parallel	Serial
Advanced Technology Attachment or ATA (aka PATA, IDE, EIDE, ATAPI, etc.) disk/tape peripheral attachment bus the original ATA is parallel, but see also the recent serial ATA)	USB Universal Serial Bus, used for a variety of external devices
HIPPI High Performance Parallel Interface	Serial Attached SCSI and other serial SCSI buses
IEEE-488 (also called GPIB, General-Purpose Instrumentation Bus, and HPIB, Hewlett-Packard Instrumentation Bus)	Serial ATA
PC card, previously known as PCMCIA, much used in laptop computers and other portables, but fading with the introduction of USB and built-in network and modem connections	Controller Area Network ("CAN bus")
SCSI Small Computer System Interface, disk/tape peripheral attachment bus	EIA-485
	FireWire

Peripheral Component Interface (PCI) Bus

As mentioned earlier in the chapter the PCI is a popular peripheral bus used in the PC range for high speed I/O subsystems such as graphics display adapters, NICs, disk controllers etc. The PCI bus connects expansion cards and drives to the CPU and other sub systems. On most systems the bus speed of the PCI bus is 33MHz. If a higher speed is used then cards, drives, and other devices need to support the higher speed. The exception to this is found in some servers, which are equipped with 64-bit (extra wide) 66MHz PCI slots that can accept high-speed cards.

The PCI is designed to support both single and multi-processor systems and utilises synchronous timing. Version is PCI 2.2 and supports up to 64 data lines at 66MHz, which assuming one bit transfers with one cycle, gives transfer rates of: 64*66M=4.224 GBps, or 528 Mbytes/s. Part of the reason it is popular is because the PCI bus requires very few chips to implement and supports other buses. Additionally, because the specification is in the public domain and it is supported by a broad section of microprocessor industry, PCI products from different vendors are compatible. For this reason we will discuss the PCI bus in more detail next. Version 3.0 is an evolutionary release of the PCI specification that includes edits to provide better readability and incorporate

Engineering Change Notices (ECNs) that have been developed since the release of version 2.3. The Conventional PCI 3.0 specification also completes the migration to 3.3V-only slots by removing support for 5.0V only keyed add-in cards. Version 3.0 is the current standard for Conventional PCI, to which vendors should be developing products. [21]

Bus Structure: PCI can be configured as a 32-bit or 64-bit bus. It utilises synchronous timing and activity occurs in the form of transaction between a master and target. When a bus master takes control of the bus, it determines the type of transaction that will occur next. Figure 4.10 shows the timing waveform for a PCI read cycle. Here it can be seen that during the address phase of the transaction the control/byte enable pins are used to signal the transaction type. Some of the commands are as follows,

INTA: PCI Bus interrupt controller signal, address lines are not used and the byte enable lines contain the interrupt type number.

Special Cycle: Used by the master to broadcast to one or more targets.

I/O Read/ Write: Used to transfer data between master and slave.

Memory READ/WRITE: These specify the transfer of a burst of data, occurring one or more clock cycles

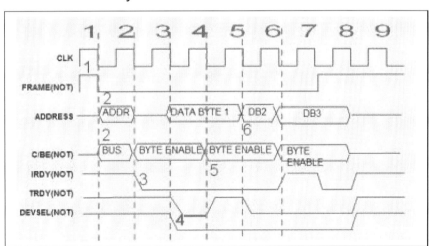

Figure 4.10. PCI READ cycle timing

Following the timing sequence in Figure 4.10 with points labelled 1-6:

1. Frame signal is active low and activates at the falling edge of the first clock cycle. This signal remains active until the last data phase.

2. Address is edge triggered by Frame signal and the address bus carries the address of the instruction. At the same time Control is enabled on the C/BE line and this multiplexed control bus takes the bus control signal.

3. Next change occurs during clock 2. Input signal IRDY is triggered causing the data byte to be enabled on the control bus. (BYTE ENABLE).

4. During the next clock pulse address of DATA BYTE 1 is placed on the address bus and the device select is enabled for a read operation.

5. The read proceeds until the next pulse when byte enable is renewed. However the first data byte DATA BYTE 1 is not complete and TRDY is revoked until the next (5th) clock.

6. At this point DB2 is read and the next byte enabled reads in byte

Accelerated Graphics Port (AGP)

The need for Intel has pioneered increased bandwidth between the main processor and the video subsystem, a new interface, designed specifically for the video subsystem. It is called the Accelerated Graphics Port or AGP.

As software evolves and computer use continues into previously unexplored areas such as 3D acceleration and full-motion video playback, both the processor and the video chipset need to process more and more information. The PCI bus is reaching its performance limits in these applications, especially with hard disks and other peripherals also competing for the same bandwidth.

Another issue has been the increasing demands for video memory. As 3D computing becomes more mainstream, much larger amounts of memory become required, not just for the screen image but also for doing the 3D calculations. This traditionally has meant putting more memory on the video card for doing this work. There are two problems with this:

Cost: Video card memory is very expensive compared to regular system RAM.

Limited Size: The amount of memory on the video card is limited: if you decide to put 6 MB on the card and you need 4 MB for the frame buffer, you have 2 MB left over for processing work and that's it (unless you do a hardware upgrade). It's not easy to expand this memory, and you can't use it for anything else if you don't need it for video processing.

AGP overcomes these problems by allowing the video processor to access the main system memory for doing its calculations. This is more efficient because this memory can be shared dynamically between the system processor and the video processor, depending on the needs of the system.

The idea behind AGP is simple: create a faster, dedicated interface between the video chipset and the system processor. The interface is only between these two devices; this has three major advantages: it makes it easier to implement the port, makes it easier to increase AGP in speed, and makes it possible to put enhancements into the design that are specific to video.

AGP is considered a port, and not a bus, because it only involves two devices (the processor and video card) and is not expandable.

One of the great advantages of AGP is that it isolates the video subsystem from the rest of the PC so there isn't nearly as much contention over I/O bandwidth as there is with PCI. With the video card removed from the PCI bus, other PCI devices will also benefit from improved bandwidth.

AGP Interface

The AGP specification is based on the PCI 2.1 specification, which includes a high-bandwidth 66 MHz speed. AGP bus connects the video card directly to main memory and processor. It is very high speed compared to standard PCI and has a standard speed of 66MHz. Only one device can be hooked to the AGP bus as it only supports one video card so the running speed is even better compared to the PCI bus, which has many devices on it at once. AGP is a Point-to-Point bus using 1.5 Volt or 3.3V signalling. (Note: lower voltage swing improves speed). The AGP specification adds 20 additional signals not included in the PCI bus. It defines the Protocol, Electrical and Mechanical aspects of the bus. [22]

AGP Bus Width, Speed and Bandwidth

The AGP data bus may be 8, 16, 24, 32, or 64 bits wide, but unlike the PCI, which runs at half of the system bus speed, it runs at full bus speed. This means that on a standard Pentium II motherboard AGP runs at 66 MHz instead of the PCI bus's 33 MHz. This of course immediately doubles the bandwidth of the port; instead of the limit of 127.2 MB/s as with PCI, AGP in its lowest speed mode has a bandwidth of 254.3 MB/s. Plus of course the benefits of not having to share bandwidth with other PCI devices. In addition to doubling the speed of the bus, AGP has defined a 2X mode, which uses special signalling to allow twice as much data to be sent over the port at the same clock speed.

What the hardware does is to send information on both the rising and falling edges of the clock signal. Each cycle, the clock signal transitions from "0", to "1" ("rising edge"), and back to "0" ("falling edge"). While PCI for example only transfers data on one of these transitions each cycle, AGP transfers data on both. The result is that the performance doubles again, to 508.6 MB/s theoretical bandwidth. So it is seen that with the base clock rate of 66MHz, to achieve to 2x, 4x, and 8x speeds the clock is doubled each time. AGP uses both edges of the clock to transfer data. The resulting performance is as follows,

- AGP (1x): 66MHz clock, 8 bytes/clock, Bandwidth: 266MB/s [3.3V or 1.5V signal swing]
- AGP 2x: 133MHz clock, 8 bytes/clock, Bandwidth: 533MB/s [3.3V or 1.5V signal swing]
- AGP 4x: 266MHz clock, 16 bytes/clock, Bandwidth: 1066MB/s [1.5V signal swing]
- AGP 8x: 533MHz clock, 32 bytes/clock, Bandwidth: 2.1GB/s [0.8V signal swing], still uses 1.5 volt motherboard power

AGP Video Pipelining

One performance enhancing benefit of AGP is its ability to pipeline requests for data. Pipelining was first used by modern processors as a way to improve performance by letting the sequential parts of tasks overlap; see here for a full description of how it works. With AGP, the video chipset can use a similar technique when requesting information from memory, which improves performance.

4.6. The System Clock

The system clock is used to time all bus activity. Typically it is the speed of the frontside bus without any enhancements (such as double pumping, or quad pumping) on it. The PCI bus speed is determined from the system clock via the use of a divider. In most systems PCI dividers are set automatically and cannot be altered. The three most common dividers built in to motherboards are: 1/5 (used on a 166MHz system clock), 1/4 (used on a 133MHz system clock), and 1/3 used on a 100MHz system clock. A 1/6 divider is sometimes available for over clocking and future support. For example: If the system clock is 166MHz and a 1/5 divider is set in the motherboard's bios then the PCI bus speed would be 166/5 = ~33MHz.

System clock and processor speed

The processor speed is determined by a multiplier, which is built into the CPU. The processor speed is calculated by multiplying the system clock with this multiplier. The CPU has its multiplier hard wired in to the chip, and this cannot be changed. On the other hand the system clock can be set on the motherboard by using the BIOS or switches on the board itself.

4.7. Bus performance

Buses communicate data and this in turn encounters data propagation delays. The more devices that we attach to a bus, the longer the delays will be in propagating this data. With more devices attached the increase in currents on the bus will raise temperature and this will further restrict performance.

Furthermore, with a large number of devices, the aggregate demand for access to the bus from all devices connected to the bus causes excess loads.

In order to avoid bottlenecks, multiple buses are used in most systems providing a hierarchy of buses each operating at different levels and characteristics. In the hierarchical arrangement of buses the high-speed buses are used to access components close to the processor and the slower-speed buses provide access to components farther away from the processor.

In the vast majority, data communication occurs between individual devices, and this means that only one device can place data on the bus at any one time. In the same way the device that this data is destined for is the only device that accesses the data. A dedicated circuit is needed to ensure that this happens and this is part of the so-called bus arbitration, which is the process of ensuring that only one device places information onto the bus at any one time.

Typically bus arbitration is implemented using the master-slave principle where the master is given control of the bus and can place information onto it. The slave receives the information from the master and a process of acknowledgement ensues. Both the master and the slave support a common communication protocol. The main methods of arbitration are classified as being either centralised or decentralised. With centralised systems, a dedicated central bus controller mediates all device requests for the bus. In the decentralised system there is no dedicated controller and devices are selected in accordance with a protocol.

Bus communication

All communication between devices requires that signals be placed on the bus. These signals will cause some devices to operate in a certain way. For example, a chip select (CS) pin going low will activate a chip for access. Once the chip is activated, it can be used to communicate data. When there are a large number of devices and when a number of signals have to be processed the question of timing the occurrence of these becomes an issue. Timing with buses is classified into two types, namely synchronous and asynchronous. Although both require a reference to the system clock, there is a difference in how they operate.

Synchronous buses: Figure 4.11 shows the principle of synchronous bus communication. Here the clock determines the occurrence of events on the bus and typically all events start at the beginning of a clock cycle. The essence of this is that the sequence or the order in which signals are processed is pre-determined. An example of a synchronous bus is the PCI bus. Figure 4.11 shows that in synchronous communications the start, address and read signals occur one clock cycle before data and acknowledge signals. This is pre-defined and implemented on a synchronous bus.

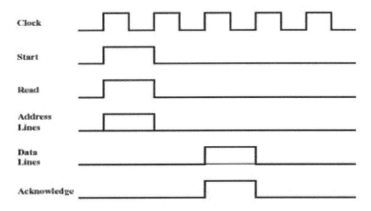

Figure 4.11. Synchronous communication diagram

Asynchronous buses: With asynchronous buses signals are not timed to occur in a particular way. Rather it is the occurrence of one event that follows and depends on the occurrence of a previous event and NOT on some timing requirement. This is shown in Figure 4.11 where it is seen that signals trigger other signals. (i.e. MSYN triggers SSYN and data lines on the rising edge, and also that SSYN triggers the address and read signals on the falling edge). An asynchronous bus has no master clock; instead, it uses a handshake protocol between a master and a slave device. Thus asynchronous buses are event driven rather than synchronised to a clock. It has to be said that even so, the event is still co-ordinated by clock transitions, which is an electronic requirement, but the clock does not control when the events occur. This is more flexible than synchronous bus but more complicated as well. It accommodates wider range of device speeds. Example: VMEbus, Futurebus+

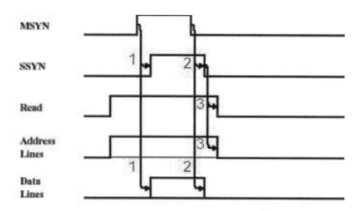

Figure 4.12. Asynchronous communication diagram

Bus characteristics

Perhaps the most commonly encountered characteristic of the bus is the bus width. This is typically associated with parallel buses and refers to the number of bits that are arranged in parallel. The wider the data bus the more bits can be transferred at one time. For example: 4K bytes need to be transferred from ROM to RAM. Assume for the sake of argument that the CPU instruction to move this data from ROM to RAM requires 10 Clocks to execute. If the data bus is 16 bits wide, and the processor speed is 1GHz, the transfer will be complete in: (4096/2*10)/1GHz=20mS. For a data bus which is 32 bits wide the same transfer will complete in: (4096/4*10)/1GHz=10mS.

The width of the address bus determines the size of the address space that can be accessed at any one time. Thus, the wider the address bus the greater the range of addresses that can be accessed at any one time. For example: An address bus 16bits wide will be able to access 2^{16}=64K locations while a 32-bit wide bus will be able to access 2^{32}=4G locations.

Data transfer type

When data is transferred on the bus a number of different transfer types can be identified. In all cases it is necessary to identify the address of the data and also the control signal and all buses are designed to support both write and read operations. In many cases buses are multiplexed so that chip space is minimised. For example, multiplexed address/data buses use the bus first to obtain the address of the data and then use it to carry the data itself. Where the address bus is dedicated (NOT-multiplexed) once placed on the bus, the address remains there while data are placed onto the data bus.

Typically, for WRITE operations, data is placed as soon as bus is stable and for READ operations the data needs to be fetched first and so there is a certain amount of delay. For this reason a wait state usually precedes a READ operation while the data is being fetched from its location. For either a READ or a WRITE there may be delays due to arbitration since there are a number of sequences that need to be performed. For example, first seize the bus to request the READ or WRITE, then seize the bus to perform the READ or WRITE. For combined operations such as READ, WRITE operations the following main types are identified.

1. **Read-Modify-Write**: The address is used for the READ and is retained for the immediate WRITE to the same location. This is used to protect shared memory in multiprogramming systems. The sequence from left to right is shown below.

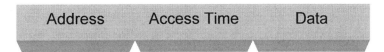

2. **Read-After-Write**: After WRITE perform immediate READ to check if the value is valid. The sequence from left to right is shown below.

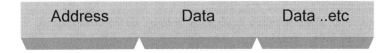

3. **Block Data Transfer**: Some bus systems also support block data transfer, which means that after the first address cycle, there follows a burst on n data cycles. This presumes that the data, which is being transferred, is in made up on n blocks. The sequence from left to right is shown below.

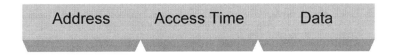

Exercises

4.1. How do longer buses affect bus speeds?

4.2. How does the addition of more chips to the bus affect bus performance?

4.3. How does the loading improve if we introduce multiple buses?

4.4. What two benefits are afforded by the hierarchical bus arrangement?

4.5. What is bus arbitration?

4.6. Explain the master-slave principle in bus arbitration.

4.7. Describe two methods of bus arbitration.

4.8. What is the difference between synchronous and asynchronous bus timing?

4.9. You have two separate systems, one with a 16-bit data bus, another is 32 bits wide, and both systems are running at 1GHz. If a MOV instruction takes 10 clocks, calculate how much time it would take each system to transfer 4Kbytes of data.

4.10. How does the size of the address bus affect system performance?

4.11. Explain the SCSI standard including the variations and suggest typical applications.

4.12. True or False:

    a) All buses support both read and write operations

    b) Addresses are stored on the data bus

    c) Data are stored on the data bus indefinitely

    d) Address and data buses cannot be multiplexed.

    e) You can not write to RAM only to ROM

    f) You can not read from ROM only from RAM

    g) A Wait state usually precedes a READ operation

    h) There is no Wait state for a WRITE operation

    i) A dedicated address bus retains the address while data are placed on the address bus

    j) A multiplexed data/address bus allows both data and address bus operations to be shared, by timing these to occur during different clock cycles.

4.13. Discuss the main limitations of SCSI.

4.14. Explain how the LVD drive can improve SCSI performance.

4.15. List some of the present day internal and external buses and suggest their applications.

4.16. Explain the combined operations and where they can be used: 1) Read-Modify-Write 2) Read-After-Write 3) Block data transfer

4.17. What is the PCI Bus used for?

4.18. What is the current version of the PCI bus?

4.19. How many data lines can a PCI support and at what speed?

4.20. What is the maximum data throughput?

4.21. What timing is used in the PCI Synchronous or Asynchronous?

4.22. Does PCI support multi-processor systems?

4.23. When does the PCI decide on what transaction type is required?

4.24. What is the INTA pulse used during PCI cycle?

4.25. What is the Special Cycle?

4.26. What are bridges used in PCI?

CHAPTER 5 CPU DESIGN

5.1. Introduction

All CPUs are integrated digital electronic circuits and the internal working of the constituent parts is controlled by digital signals sent along internal buses. The execution of a program begins by fetching an instruction from memory and then placing it inside the execution unit. All instructions follow this pattern and the Fetch-Execute cycle keeps repeating, each time fetching the next instruction in the sequence, until the program terminates. When an instruction is fetched, it is temporarily stored in a buffer register and in order to be executed in needs to be passed on the control unit. The control unit has an instruction register (IR) to store the instruction so that it can be processed. The designers of the CPU prescribe the digital logic operations that the control unit applies in order to decode the instruction. Typically different bits in the IR will represent the variants that the instruction can take. For example, if the CPU is 8-bit and the designer decides to support up to 8 instructions, then 3 bits are sufficient to identify these (i.e. $2^3=8$). The other 5 bits can be used to describe the type of addressing mode that is used in this instruction and the data that will be operated on (i.e. the Operand).

The size of the data bus determines the size of the registers used. Thus an 8-bit CPU will have 8-bit data bus and all of its registers will be 8-bit. If the data bus is 32-bit then the same principle applies, and more hardware is needed to implement the registers and the associated internal functions of the CPU. For this reason and due to the large number of internal components, wider buses require large chip areas and in this case the heat dissipation of the CPU becomes an issue. In this chapter we will consider some aspects that relate to the design of a CPU. We will also consider the basic principle of operation of a typical CPU so that the considerations needed for design can become clear.

Digital circuit control

The internal structure of a CPU is a complex arrangement of digital electronic circuits. For example registers inside the CPU are made up of Flip-Flops (FFs), which are electronic transistor circuits that transfer the value, which is present at the input to the output after a clock signal is received on the clock input. (See appendix 1). Thus in an 8-bit CPU each register is a set of eight flip-flops (FF) with each FF representing one bit (8 bits=byte, 2 bytes=16 bits = word, 2 words=32 bits = double word). These FFs are active devices (i.e. they consume power) and they retain the values as long as there is power in the circuit. Furthermore, they do not need to be refreshed in the way that DRAM is.

The control circuitry is located inside the control unit (CU), which coordinates all CPU activity. By controlling clock inputs to devices, the required sequence of events is maintained for the processing task. The control unit decodes the instruction bits and issues control signals to components inside the CPU as well as those outside it, in order to control the processing. Thus each CPU has a control unit to decode the instructions, which that particular CPU is designed to support. For this reason every family of CPUs is different and each has an instruction set that has been specifically designed for it. Designing the instruction set is therefore one of the first tasks of a CPU designer.

5.2. Instruction set

To design a CPU we need to consider the number of instructions that we wish to support. It is worth noting at this point that instruction set design falls into two main categories, namely Complex instruction set computers (CISC) and reduced Instruction Set Computers (RISC). More on this later, but as a summary and in a very broad sense it can be said that CISC architecture aims to implement computers that support a large number of instructions, which can be arranged to describe complex processing sequences. Conversely RISC implement a limited instruction set, but these are designed to work on many processors that are arranged in parallel and are therefore able to execute these simple instructions concurrently. Both approaches are valid and to a large extent they complement each other. Design of the instruction set is therefore a major part of CPU design. We will consider this next, with reference to CISC computers but the general approach is equally valid for RISC. (More details are given in Chapter 6 of this text)

Instruction set design

Typically in a computer system each instruction must contain 4 basic components:

1. **Operation code (Op-code)**: this specifies the operation to be performed and it is expressed as a binary code consisting of a prescribed number of bits. Every instruction must have a unique Opcode.

2. **Source Operand reference**: Operands required for the instruction must be specified. An Operand can be passed directly with the instruction (i.e. direct addressing) or it can be supplied through an address, which contains the value to be used (indirect addressing).

3. **Result reference**: This describes where the result of the operation should be placed. Once again this can be direct or indirect depending on whether the value is supplied directly or though an address reference.

4. **Next instruction reference:** This provides information about how and where the next instruction is obtained.

Different computer applications require different instructions and therefore designers must consider the requirements and based on these propose a design solution. In all cases an instruction set should be functionally complete and should permit the user to formulate any high-level data processing task, which the application must support. The basic categories of instructions and a brief description are shown in Table 5.1.

Table 5.1 Five categories of instructions

1. **Arithmetic operations**	2. **Logic operations**	3. **Data movement**	4. **I/O (data movements**	5. **Control operations**

ADD AL,03H
SUB AL,BL
MUL AL,03
DIV AL,02
	Boolean
	AND AL,BL
	XOR AL,55H
		Internal to the system
		MOV AL,BL
			Between the computer and external devices
			OUT DX,AX
				CALL, JMP

Instruction address types

All computer programs contain a number of instructions that need to execute and typically these instructions reference data that needs to be processed. The data that is required is referred to as the operand, and all instructions must include a description of how this operand ill be addressed and this is referred to as the addressing mode. The first byte of any program must include an Opcode, reference to the operand and also an identifier for the addressing mode. These are typically fields within the byte that are defined at the time that the instruction set was designed. Figure 5.1 shows an example of fields in an 8-bit CPU. This design provides three bits for the Opcode, one bit for addressing mode and four bits for the operand.

The three bits on the left are used to identify a unique Opcode and for this Opcode if the address bit (B4) is 1 then the Operand is included in the byte and it is passed directly with the instruction. (i.e. direct addressing mode). If on the other hand the value of B4 is 0, then the addressing mode is indirect, and the value of the Operand is found in the memory address to which the Operand field points. In Figure 5.1 this value is in memory location [8], and the data value stored there is FE in hexadecimal. Note that for this CPU the highest value of the Operand when using direct addressing is 0F, which is a limitation imposed by the number of bits used to specify it (i.e. $2^4=16$). But if a larger number is needed then it can be stored in memory and accessed indirectly through one of the 16 memory addresses that a 4-bit Operand address can access. In this case values can range 0-FF (i.e. $2^8=256$).

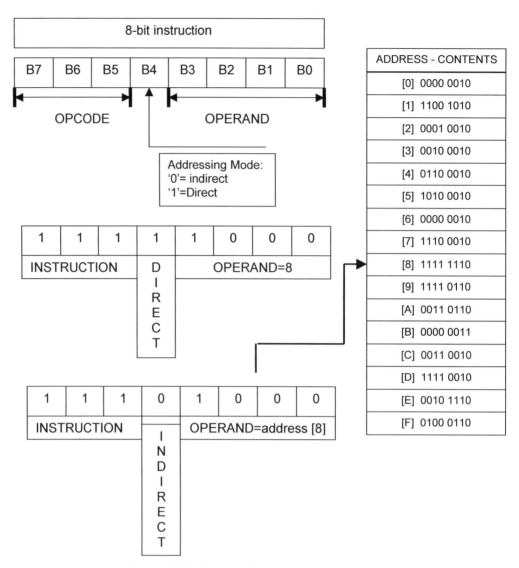

Figure 5.1. Instruction format examples

From the above it can be deduced that whatever the processing requirement, there needs to be a method of addressing the information that is needed for the instruction to execute. We consider the different address types next.

3 address instructions

In typical arithmetic or logical instructions, 3 addresses are required; namely, 2 for the Operands and one for the result. The format is as follows,

X (result) = Y (First Operand) + Z (Second Operand)

These addresses can be explicitly given or implied by the instruction. With increasing memory speeds (due to caching) this arrangement offers a high degree of flexibility to the compiler. Furthermore, it reduces the need for keeping items in registers because it uses three addresses to store all the values that are being used. Since three addresses accompany an instruction this approach is a fraction slower than the alternatives that use fewer addresses. This format is rarely used in general-purpose computers due to the length of addresses themselves and the resulting length of the instruction words.

2 address instructions

Here two addresses are used and one of these is used to specify both an Operand and the result location. i.e.

$$X = X + Y.$$

Thus the result address is multiplexed with one of the Operand addresses and the result overwrites the corresponding Operand value. This model is very common in instruction sets because it uses fewer addresses and this is possible because it is often not necessary to retain the values of both Operands.

1-address instructions

Here only one address of one Operand is supplied because the operation involves a register. This is only possible with the accumulator register, which does not need to be specified with an address. However, two addresses are implied in the instruction. Instructions of this type are traditional accumulator-based operations, i.e.

$$Acc = Acc + X$$

0 address instructions

This relies on use of registers only and no access to address bus is made directly. All addresses are implied, as in register-based operations i.e.

TBA (transfer register B to A)

As a result these operations are very fast but they cannot be used to provide long-term storage.

Stack-based operations

Here all operations are based on the use of a stack in memory to store bytes of code. This can be very quick since the stack operations of PUSH and POP need very few clock cycles. By pushing a predetermined sequence of instructions onto the stack, a very efficient algorithm can be made to execute from the stack. Note that all work with the stack is using PUSH and POP operations. (Refer to stack description in Chapter 1).

5.3. Basic CPU operation

As mentioned earlier the CPU is responsible for fetching program instructions from memory, decoding the instruction, executing the instruction and transferring data to/from memory or IO. These tasks are performed in accordance with the programme, which comprises a list of instructions to be executed. All instructions are processed as binary values, however it is common to represent these values as hexadecimal code for convenience. Figure 5.2 shows an example of instructions to add a number to the accumulator for the Intel x86 family of processors.

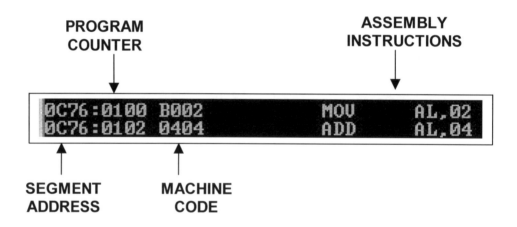

Figure 5.2. Instructions to add a value to accumulator

In figure 5.1 the first byte that the CPU sees is B0 and this is the instruction that is located at address 0100 as pointed to by the programme counter register. (Intel calls this the instruction pointer (IP) register). The instruction at this memory address is MOV AL,02, in assembly language. The machine code for this instruction is B002. The instruction is to move directly into the accumulator the value that follows in the next byte (i.e. 02). When this instruction completes the PC is incremented so that it points to the next instruction to be executed. In this case the next instruction is ADD that starts with the byte 04, followed by the value to be added (i.e. 04). Note that the PC at this time points to location 102, which means that the first instruction has used up 2 bytes in code memory. This shows that incrementing the PC does not necessarily mean moving to the next memory location, rather it means moving to the location of the next instruction in memory.

It is seen from Figure 5.3 that the program starts at location 0100 where the first byte B0 is stored. To its right follow the sequence of bytes that constitute the instructions. If the program counter register is set at 0100 then the program runs as normal and executes successfully as shown at the top of the figure. If for arguments sake the program counter is set at 0101,which we know to be data value 02, it is seen from Figure 5.3 that the CPU interprets the code completely differently and assumes that 02 is the instruction to ADD. The program cannot execute normally because it does not execute what is required. (See bottom of Figure 5.3)

```
0C76:0100 B002          MOV      AL,02
0C76:0102 0404          ADD      AL,04
0C76:0104 CD21          INT      21
```

Code starting at address 0100 shows the desired assembly statements on the right

```
AX=0006  BX=0000  CX=0000  DX=0000  SP=FFEE  BP=0000  SI=
DS=0C76  ES=0C76  SS=0C76  CS=0C76  IP=0100     NV UP EI PL
0C76:0100 B002          MOV      AL,02
-g=100

Program terminated normally
```

Running the program from address 0100 executes successfully

```
0C76:0101 0204          ADD      AL,[SI]
0C76:0103 04CD          ADD      AL,CD
0C76:0105 2193D0C0      AND      [BP+DI+C0D0],DX
```

Code starting at address 0101 shows the assembly statements on the right that are not as desired, and the programme cannot execute normally. It will execute but the results will not be as desired, which defeats the objective of programming.

Figure 5.3. PC points to the first instruction of the program

When a programme is loaded for execution, the first byte is always considered to be an instruction. That is to say it cannot be data. The composition of the first byte contains information on how the next byte (if there are any) of the instruction will be obtained. (i.e. next instruction reference)

Programmers view

Figure 5.4 shows which of the areas supported by CPU are accessible to programmers. Notwithstanding the different levels of programming it is seen that programmers have access to applications, high-level language support, the operating system as well as assembly and machine code. At each of these levels programmers can write programs that are interpreted, compiled or assembled into executable machine code. At the heart of the CPU is the digital logic, to which programmers have no access. This is driven by a microprogram of instructions that are embedded within the CPU and cannot be modified except by a new design and production of the chip. This logic is hardwired inside the CPU and the microprogrammed instructions control the internal operation of the CPU.

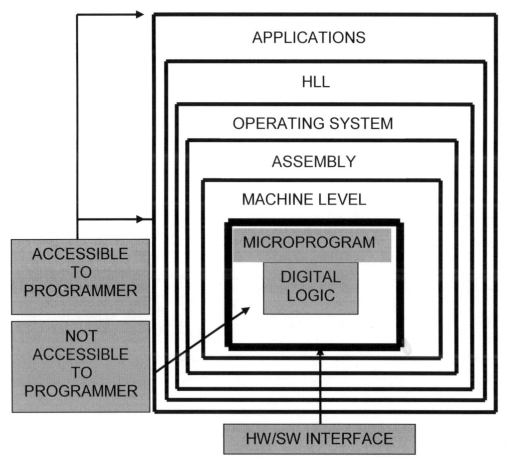

Figure 5.4. Programming access to the CPU

The programming of instructions is typically concerned with obtaining a result after the sequence of instructions have executed. This involves programming the CPU to perform tasks by READ/WRITE operations to and from memory and performing some arithmetic operation. For example, in order to calculate the area of a circle, the CPU needs to be instructed to obtain the values for the radius variable (r), the constant (pi) and to perform the calculation of the area in accordance with the prescribed formula. The read and write operations to do this are shown in Figure 5.5. Here it is seen that the CPU must read some data and also write other data. The actual processing is done inside the CPU where the calculation is performed.

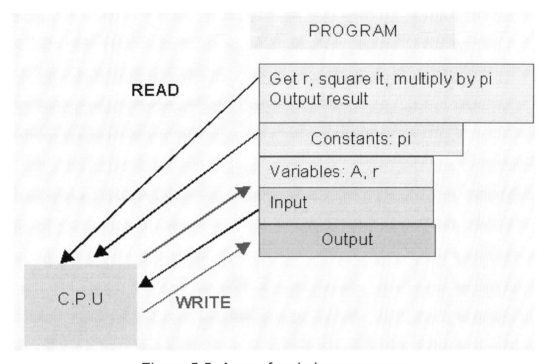

Figure 5.5. Area of a circle programme

In order to describe the instructions given to the CPU without specifically using a programming language it is common to use a symbolic representation referred to as Register Transfer Language (RTL). This is not a programming language; rather it is a notation for describing the instructions given to the CPU. A brief description is provided next.

Rules for using Register Transfer Language (RTL)

Direction is RIGHT to LEFT, that is to say, to move data from register B to register A we would write [A] ← [B]

We introduce comments after the semi-colon ";"

Square brackets [ ] indicate location, For example:

[D0] =MONDAY ; The register D0 contains the value MONDAY. The square brackets here indicate the address of the register D0, which will be loaded with the value MONDAY.

[MAR]? [PC]   ;Copy contents of PC to MAR

[3]? [5]   ;Copy contents of Location 5 to Location 3

[PC? [PC]+1   ;Increment PC

[M(5)]? [PC]   ;Copy PC to memory address 5

[M(20)] = 6   ;States that memory (20) is equal to 6

[M(20)]? 6   ;Number 6 is placed in M(20)

[M(20)]? [M(6)] ;Contents of location (6) are copied into location (20)

[M(20)]? [M(6)]+3   ;Read location (6) add 3 and store result in location (20)

As an example consider how RTL can be used to represent a Fetch cycle.

[MAR]←[PC] ;Copy contents of PC to MAR

[PC] ←[PC]+1 ;Increment PC

[MBR]←[M9[MAR])] ;Read the instruction from memory

[IR]←[MBR]   ;Move instructions to IR

CU ←[IR(opcode)] ;Transmit Opcode to Control Unit

Note that the Control Unit (CU) is used to decode the instruction, which is in the instruction register (IR). In other words the CU interprets the bit pattern and translates this into a sequence of actions taking place during the execution of the instruction.

5.4.   Internal functioning of the CPU

Figure 5.6 shows the basic arrangement of components inside a typical CPU. The lines connecting the internal components represent highways along which signals flow from one part of the CPU to another. Here these are shown as single lines, but in reality these would be made up of many parallel

113

connections, which is equal to the number of bits in CPU registers. As mentioned earlier the program counter is a special register that keeps track of the next instruction to be executed. It is incremented to point to the next instruction as soon as the instruction that is current has been passed onto the memory address register (MAR). The contents of MAR are stored in a temporary register called the memory buffer register (MBR) and from here the instruction is diverted to the Instruction Register (IR) and when data is available it is sent to the arithmetic and logic unit. The data register is used for storing temporary results. As the name implies the arithmetic and logic unit (ALU) performs arithmetic and logic operations.

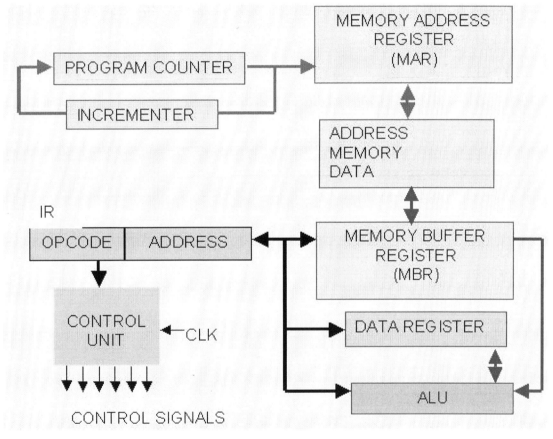

Figure 5.6. Internal components of a CPU

The instruction register (IR) supplies the instruction to the control unit, which contains the digital circuit that decodes the instruction in accordance with the way that the instruction set has been designed.

Communication of information between the various components is controlled by clocked D-type flip-flops (FF), which make up the registers, and gates that open and close depending on the signal applied to them. A D-type flip-flop has a single input D and after it is clocked this input is transferred to the outputs Q and Q (NOT). The outputs Q and Q (NOT) can be fed into other flip-flops so that the bits are transferred between these devices. There is a separate flip-flop for every bit; so if a register is 8-bit, then 8 separate flip-flops are required. They are arranged in parallel and are clocked at the same time so that the complete byte can be transferred. Figure 5.6 shows a simplified diagram of how D-type flip-flops can be used to transfer data. Here the input D is seen to start at a high level '1' when the FF is clocked at time 1, the output follows the input D and the output Q goes high, at the same time output Q (NOT) goes low. This state remains until the next change in input D, which happens at time 3. At this time the input D is set to low, and the FF clocked again. As a result the outputs Q and Q (NOT) become low and high respectively.

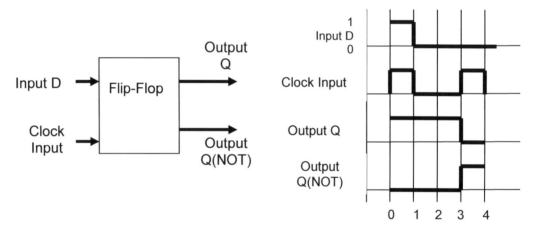

Figure 5.6. Clocking D-Type flip-flops

If a number of these FFs are connected so that the output of one is the input to another, and so on, then a series of FFs can be clocked to control the flow of data. A simplified diagram is shown in Figure 5.7. The diagram should only serve to illustrate how clocking FFs can transfer bits; it does not make any real statement about the sequence that is carried out.

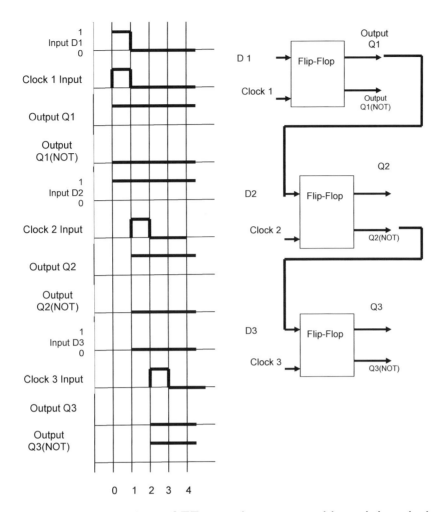

Figure 5.7. A number of FFs can be arranged in a daisy chain

To illustrate how this principle applies to the internal operation of a CPU Figure 5.8 shows the arrangement of the various registers that are used in the processing of instructions. Each register is shown as a FF and of course there should be as many FFs as there are bits in a register, although the figure shows only one for convenience. Furthermore, Figure 5.8 shows that gates (G1→n) (switched independently) are used to deliver signal outputs to the inputs of the next FF. The sequence of switching the gates and clocking the FF determines how bits are transferred inside the CPU. In order to illustrate the internal operations Figure 5.9 provides an example of the instruction ADD [Address value] to data register D0, described as a sequence using RTL. Here the clocking of FFs and the switching of gates as numbered are also shown in the comments.

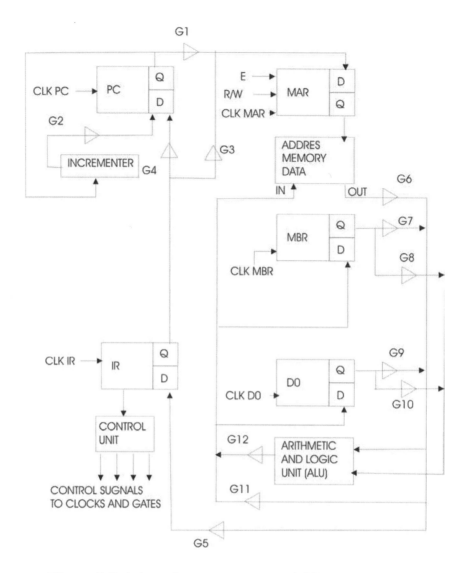

Figure 5.8. Internal arrangements of CPU components

With reference to Figure 5.9, the starting point of execution is the register PC where the instruction to be executed is held. The contents of the PC are placed onto the memory address register (MAR). This is done by switching gate 1 (G1) and clocking MAR. The following RTL describes the sequence, which should be fairly self-explanatory.

```
EXAMPLE: MODEL THE INSTRUCTION:  ADD <ADDRESS>, D0

1        [MAR] ← [PC]; ENABLE G1, clock MAR
1a.      INC ← [PC]
2        [PC] ← INC; Enable G2, clock PC
3        [MBR] ← [M([MAR])] Enable Memory (E), R/W = 1, enable G6, G11, clock MBR.
Here we are reading memory at address given by MAR and transferring it to MBR. Thus
memory READ is enabled, data is output through G6 and G11 into the data register of
MBR.
4        [IR] ← [MBR]; enable G8, clock IR
4a       CU ← [IR(OPCODE)] ;Here IR contains the instruction and passes it onto the CU.
         Clocking G3 places this into MAR. MAR needs the address of the operand, CU
         needs the opcode.
5        [MAR] ←[IR(address)] enable G3, clock  MAR ;clocking MAR moves instruction to
memory.
6        [MBR] ← [M(MAR)]; enable memory (E), R/W = 1,  enable G6, G11, clock MBR (as
in 3 above)
7        ALU ←[MBR] enable G7 ;data to D0
7a       ALU ← [D0] enable G10 ;data to ALU
8        [DQ] ←[ALU] enable G12, clock D0 ;output result to D0
```

Figure 5.9. RTL description with clock and gating signals

5.5. The Microprogram

With reference to Figure 5.8, when the clock pulses a register (FFs), the
D input of each register is transferred to output Q where it remains until the
next clock pulse. The output from any register can be gated onto the bus by
enabling the appropriate gate (G1–G12). Note that the gate is actually a digital
circuit called a tri-state buffer. This is a 3-state device where the states are
ON, OFF and Open-Circuit (O/C). These are very useful because the O/C
state requires no current and therefore it is more energy efficient than
conventional 2-state gates.

If the output of the control unit is seen as signals G1-G12, Memory
signals E, R/W, and the 5 clocks going into PC, MAR, MBR, IR and D0, then
these can be modelled as a sequence of binary values generated at every new
step. We call this the Microprogram and it is shown in Figure 5.10.

STEPS	G1	G2	G3	G4	G5	G6	G7	G8	G9	G10	G11	G12	E	R/W	PC	MAR	MBR	DO	IR
1	1	0	0	0	0	0	0	0	0	0	0	0	0	X	0	1	0	0	0
2	0	1	0	0	0	0	0	0	0	0	0	0	0	X	1	0	0	0	0
3	0	0	0	0	0	1	0	0	0	0	1	0	1	1	0	0	1	0	0
4	0	0	0	0	0	0	1	0	0	0	0	0	0	0	0	0	0	0	1
5	0	0	1	0	0	0	0	0	0	0	0	0	0	0	0	1	0	0	0
6	0	0	0	0	0	1	0	0	0	0	1	0	1	1	0	0	1	0	0
7	0	0	0	0	0	0	1	0	0	1	0	0	0	0	0	0	0	0	0
8	0	0	0	0	0	0	0	0	0	0	0	1	0	0	0	0	0	1	0

The column groups above the table are labelled: GATE CONTROL SIGNAL (G1–G12), MEMORY (E, R/W), REGISTERS (PC, MAR, MBR, DO, IR).

Figure 5.10. Microcode for the sequence described in Figure 5.9.

Thus it is seen that supplying the sequence of signals to all the gates and registers at different steps results in the desired operation of individual components, which are involved in the processing of the instruction. The above is only an overview that is simplified in order to show the principle of operation of a typical CPU. More detailed description and additional reading can be found in [23,24].

Components of a Microprogrammed Control Unit

The control unit is at the heart of the CPU and it controls the processing of instructions. In other words, it is responsible for sequencing and executing microinstructions. With reference to Figure 5.10, the control unit sends the signals to gates and also clocks the FFs. Figure 5.11 shows the essential components of the CU.

The CU accepts instructions to process via the instruction register. From here instructions are fed into a decoder that determines the action to perform. The control address register includes an Address Mapper, which is a lookup table containing the starting address of the microprogram for each of the possible Opcodes. This enables the CU to translate the binary Opcode into a Microprogram bit-sequence to execute. The ALU also contains the flags that determine the state of the ALU and also the Microprogram Counter, which clocks through the stepping sequences in the microprogram and maintains a record of each step.

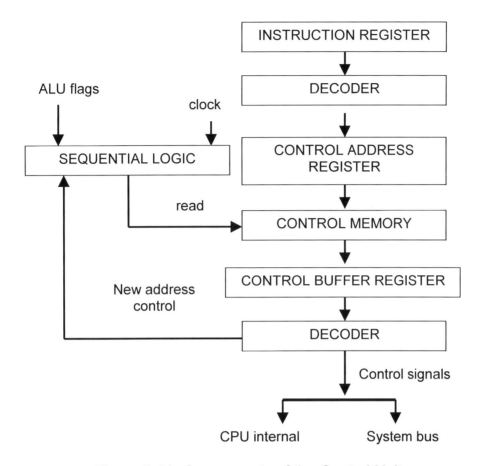

Figure 5.11. Components of the Control Unit

Control memory stores the microinstructions for execution. It is also linked to sequential logic to provide an update via a read command to the ALU. Control memory stores the complete instruction set that is supported by the CPU. In order to process any instruction, the same is transferred from control memory into the control buffer register. This register contains 4 separate fields, in order to help the CU in processing the instruction. The four fields are as follows,

1. **Next microinstruction address**, which is fed into the MAR.
2. **Microprogram counter load control field**: this determines the conditional branch to the address in the microinstruction register. i.e. branch if condition is satisfied, otherwise move on.
3. **Condition select field**: This supplies the condition to be satisfied for (2) above.

4. **CPU control field:** This field contains the most bits in the microinstruction. It controls the flow of information within the CPU by enabling the 3-state gates and clocking signals. The Microinstruction sequence control is determined by the 3 Left-Hand fields of the microinstruction register which are; NEXT ADDRESS, LOAD CONTROL, CONDITION SELECT. By loading the address into the next address field a branch can be made to anywhere in the microprogram memory. Load control tells the microprogram counter how to get the next address. Condition select field, implements the conditional branches.

The above describes the basic components of the CU. In modern computer architectures where pipelining and scaling is implemented the CU is significantly more complex, but the above should serve as a useful overview of the typical function of the CU.

5.6. Instruction set design

Designing a CPU involves a number of stages but perhaps the most important stage is the instruction set design. The instruction set architecture (ISA) defines how the internal operations of the CPU will be performed. The ISA is defined as follows,

...the attributes of a [computing] system as seem by the programmer, i.e. the conceptual structure and functional behaviour, as distinct from the organization of the data flows and controls the logic design, and the physical implementation.

- Amdahl, Blaaw, and Brooks, 1964

The issues that need to be considered for CPU design include the following,

1. **Instruction format:** The designer selects the CPU size in bits and defines the instruction set format to be used by the CPU. For the selected number of bits, it is necessary to consider how the instruction field should be broken up into its constituent parts to include the Opcode, Addressing Mode and the Operand. An example format is as follows: 3 Bits for Opcode, 1 Bit for Addressing Mode, and four Bits for Operand.

2. **Operations supported:** Decide on how many operations should be supported. As mentioned earlier consider the instruction types, i.e. arithmetic, Boolean, control transfer, logical, I/O, data transfer, jumps and decision making instructions.

3. **Registers used**: Decide on the number of registers that will be used by instructions.

4. **Addressing modes supported:** Decide on the addressing modes that will be supported. The basic ones are direct and indirect, but there are other variants such as indexed etc.

5. **Data types supported:** Consider what types of data will be supported. Most common data types include addresses, numbers, logical data and characters. Furthermore, numbers can be integers, floating point, decimal, they can be signed or unsigned etc.

Example:

Define the instruction set for 3 Bits for Opcode, 1 Bit for Addressing Mode and 4 Bits for Operand.

Solution:

Having three bits for the Opcode allows eight different instructions to be defined. One bit used for addressing means that two different addressing modes are supported. We need an instruction set that will support the following operations, arithmetic, control such as jump, load and store instructions. As an example Table 5.1 provides the different combinations of Opcode and addressing mode that make-up the upper four bits of the instruction. These bits include the 3-bit Opcode and the 1-bit addressing mode. The lower four bits are left to be assigned to either a direct value or to a memory location. From the table it is seen that this is an 8-bit CPU since the instructions are defined in 8 bits. These are listed in column 1 along with their decimal equivalent. Column 2 describes the instruction in natural language and column 3 shows the mnemonic that would typically be in assembly language. Column 4 shows the RTL expression that corresponds to the instruction.

It has to be said that the designer is in charge of the number and type of instructions to support in the CPU design. In this example we are not providing any Boolean expressions and in some cases this may well be what the design requires (although this is very unlikely). A thorough investigation of the requirements analysis must therefore be undertaken prior to design so that the end result is what is expected. In a general sense therefore the instruction set architecture design should focus on defining the following,

- Registers used
- Data transfer modes between registers, memory and I/O.
- Operations on data
- Program control operations
- Instruction set format including the decision whether or not to support variable-length and fixed-length instructions

Looking at the mnemonic description in Table 5.1 we note that some instructions use direct while others are indirectly addressed. This particular design includes a number of unconditional as well as conditional branch instructions. The reason for this would have to be due to the application requirements. For example, assume that we need to design architecture for an 8-bit CPU, which will be used in an embedded application. The application requires that a large number of input signals be compared with stored values.

The results of the comparison determine the outputs that will be produced. In this case the instruction set described in Table 5.1 is quite satisfactory. On the other hand assume that you need to design a CPU for a robotic manipulator. The position of the manipulator is controlled by 8-bit signals sent to the manipulator buffer register.

5.1. Example instruction set

Value	Instruction	Mnemonic	RTL definition
00000000 = 0	Add operand to Acc	ADD Dir N	[A]<[A]+N
00010000 = 16	Add data address contents to Acc	ADD Indir N	[A]<[A]+[M(N)]
00100000 = 32	Subtract operand from accumulator	SUB Dir N	[A]<[A]-N
00110000 = 48	Subract data address contents from Acc	SUB Indir N	[A]<[A]-[M(N)]
01000000 = 64	Load operand into Acc	LOAD Dir N	[A]<N
01010000 = 80	Load data address contents into Acc	LOAD Indir N	[A]<[M(N)]
01100000 = 96	Store Acc in data memory location	STORE Dir N	[M(N)]<[A]
01110000 = 112	Store Acc in data memory location specified by value in data memory address	STORE Indir N	[MN(N)]<[A]
10000000 = 128	Go to prog memory location	GOTO Dir N	[PC]<N
10010000 = 144	Go to prog memory location spedified by value in data memory location	GOTO Indir N	[PC]<[M(N)]
10100000 = 160	Decrement Acc by one. If Acc=Value then skip next instruction else goto next instruction.	DECSE Dir N	[A]<[A]-1 IF [A]=N THEN [PC]<[PC]+2 ELSE [PC]+1
10110000 = 176	Decrement Acc by one. If Acc=Value in data memory location then skip next instruction else goto next instruction.	DECSE Indir N	[A]<[A]-1 IF [A]=[M(N)] THEN [PC]<[PC]+2 ELSE [PC]+1
11000000 = 192	Increment Acc by one. If Acc=Value then skip next instruction else goto next instruction.	INCSE Dir N	[A]<[A]+1 IF [A]=N THEN [PC]<[PC]+2 ELSE [PC]+1
11010000 = 208	Increment Acc by one. If Acc=Value in data memory location then skip next instruction else goto next instruction.	INCSE Indir N	[A]<[A]+1 IF [A]=[M(N)] THEN [PC]<[PC]+2 ELSE [PC]+1
11100000 = 224	Skip next instruction if Acc =Value	SEQ Dir N	IF [A]=N THEN [PC]<[PC]+2 ELSE [PC]+1
11110000 = 240	Skip next instruction if Acc = Value in memory location	SEQ Indir N	IF [A]=[M(N)] THEN [PC]<[PC]+2 ELSE [PC]+1

To obtain the current position the CPU takes binary inputs via its I/O ports. In order to describe the control the CPU must apply Boolean logic analysis on all inputs. The primary logic circuits that are needed are the AND, OR, NOT and XOR gates. Well in this case the instruction set described in Table 5.1 would not be appropriate.

It should be clear that the instruction set shown in Table 5.1 could be modified to represent the desired instructions. The Opcodes would simply need to be applied to different instructions. That is to say, column 1 could remain the same, while all the other columns are changed to reflect the desired instruction set.

Once the instruction set is designed it needs to be implemented inside the CU. For every instruction the relevant Opcode must be identified and the sequence of actions that must be performed for this Opcode need to be embedded within the microprogrammed CU.

The above is only a very briefly covered example and it should be stressed that detailed design of the CPU and its internal components is a very complex task that involves significant resources, both in manpower and equipment. Modern CPU designs include multiprocessor architectures as well as parallel processing architectures. Pipelining is also extensively used to enable instructions to complete more quickly. These issues will be covered in chapters 6 and 7 of this text.

Next I introduce a simple exercise as an example of how a simple 8-CPU can be specified and designed. In the interest of keeping things simple, I have outlined only a limited requirements specification and it should be noted that these would be much more precise in an actual design project. The example therefore only serves to show the steps and some design considerations which are typically required in CPU design.

Design example: Simulating CPU Performance

This example is about designing and simulating a Central Processing unit.

Aim: To write a program that simulates the performance of an 8-bit CPU. You are required to define an instruction set, describe the simulator algorithm and write the code to implement the simulator.

Suggested Approach

1. Define the number of bits needed for an instruction set. i.e. 3 bits will support 2^3=8 instructions.

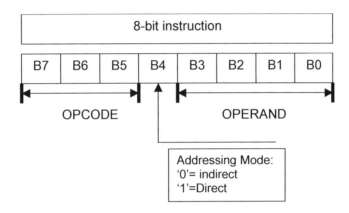

2. Select the required instructions: i.e.

Instruction	Mnemonic	RTL definition
Load Acc from memory	LDA N	[A]←[M(N)]
Store Acc in memory	STA N	[M(N)] ← [A]
Add memory to Acc.	ADD N	[A] ← [A]+[M(N)]
Branch to location N	BRA N	[PC] ← N
If A=0, Branch to location N	BEQ N	IF [A]=0 THEN [PC] ← N

3. Define the algorithm needed for simulation
4. Select a programming language i.e. (C, C++, VB6.0)
5. Design a simulator that can simulate the functionality of your CPU
6. Test your design
7. Discuss and conclude

Note: As engineers you will be required to demonstrate the ability to pick up new skills quickly and some of these will be in software development. This assignment is designed to encourage you to develop your skills in the following areas;

1. Search the range of sources for a suitable development tool.
2. Assimilate quickly to a new tool by familiarising with only the necessary components to get the work done.

3. Plan your work independently or within a group. (But free of strict supervision)
4. Documenting a software development.
5. Original design and innovation. You are encouraged to introduce original ideas provided that you can justify their use (i.e. they are not just there to show how difficult things can be).

Possible solution

CPU design involves a number of design decisions and choices. In this example we are required to write a program to simulate the performance of an 8-bit CPU. To do this we first need to define an instruction set that would be used by the CPU and use this as the basis for the development of a CPU simulator algorithm to be implemented in the C programming language.

The first stage in this development is to consider how the instruction field would be broken up into its constituent parts to make the Opcode, Addressing Mode, and Operand. The format that is suggested in this exercise will be adopted. This is because it satisfies the purpose of a basic CPU. That is to say with 3-bits 8-independent Opcodes can be produced. A single bit can be used for selecting the addressing mode and four last bits can be used for the Operand.

3 Bits for Opcode	1 Bit for Addressing Mode	Four Bits for Operand

Design

Thus we can identify the instructions that we choose to define for the CPU. Typically a CPU will be required to load an instruction into the register, thus we need to have an instruction called LOAD, and we have to associate this with a register. Assuming therefore that LDA is the load to accummulator register. What else does a CPU need to do? Well, storing a value is typically required so another instruction is to store the value of the accumulator, we can call this STA. Arithmetic operations enable the CPU to service the processing needs of users, and as a minimum we need an ADD instruction. Note that we can implement subtraction by adding negative numbers. Multiplication and division can be implemented by repetitive addition and subtraction. Therefore we need at least one instruction that can perform a decision. For example,

127

branch if equal BEQ will enable us to perform the ADD instruction until the BRA condition is satisfied.

On these basis we can define the instruction set which our CPU will support. These are only an example, and you may wish to include other instructions that you consider important. Having said that the instruction set is limited to the number of bits that you use to implement the Opcode, so if you need many more instructions you will require more than 3 bits for the Opcode. The list given in Table 5.2 shows the instructions that we will support in the simulation.

Table 5.2 Initial instruction set (direct addressing)

Value	Instruction	Mnemonic	RTL description
00000000	Load accumulator with Operand	LDA Dir N	[A]<N
00100000	Store Acc in data memory location	STORE Dir N	[M(N)]<[A]
01000000	Add data contents to Acc	ADD Dir N	[A]<[A]+N
01100000	Branch to prog memory location	BRA Dir N	[PC]<N
10000000	Compare accumulator with data and branch to prog memory location if the valuses are equal	BEQ Dir N	[A]=N?,[PC]<N
11100000	Stop execution	STOP	[PC]<STOP

Notice that the binary values shown in the left are only different in the leftmost three bits that we have identified as being the Opcode. The mnemonics listed above indicate primarily instructions with direct access to data. We differentiate between direct and indirect access by the value of the addressing mode bit. If the value of this bit is 0 then the addressing mode is direct and the value is passed with the instruction. On the other hand, for indirect addressing, the value for this bit would be 1. Repeating the instructions to include addressing information we have the expanded instruction set shown in Table 5.3, which includes indirect access to data.

Table 5.3. Indirect addressing mode

Value	Instruction	Mnemonic	RTL description
00010000	Load accumulator with Operand from memory location N	LDA InDir [N]	[A]<[N]
01010000	Add data contents of memory location N to Acc	ADD InDir N	[A]<[A]+[N]

In order to design a simulator we need to implement the registers as arrays in memory. When it is considered that four bits are used to describe the Operand, which is the value passed with the instruction, then we can have either a direct value between 0 and 15 (i.e. $2^4=16$), or we can point to 16 locations in memory that contain the data. Therefore we need to describe the registers that we will need in our simulation. These are listed in Table 5.4 with a brief explanation for each.

Table 5.4 Simulator registers

Label	Description
PC	Program counter contains the address of the next instruction to execute. This needs to be incremented after each instruction completes.
D0	This the primary data register often called the accumulator, where all the processing data is worked on.
MAR	Memory address register, stores the address of the memory location used by the instruction.
MBR	Memory buffer register, stores the information retrieved from MAR
IR	Instruction register, stores the value of the next instruction to execute
Operand	This stores the Operand part of the instruction to execute (i.e right-most four bits)
SOURCE	This stores the source of the Operand
Opcode	This stores the Opcode part of the instruction to execute (i.e left-most three bits)
AMODE	This stores the mode, which is either Direct or Indirect
MEMORY[16];	This register stores the 16 memory locations that can be indirectly accessed
RUN	This stores the program running value

Software coding

The next part of the design process is to consider how the operation of the CPU would be presented to the user so that they could understand how the CPU operates. The simulation will be written in C programming language and as an example this can be broken into three main parts as follows,

1. Display all code memory, and data memory locations. Accumulator, program counter, and next instruction. These would be displayed on the screen along with a prompt asking what type of operation to perform next.

2. A separate screen would be used to input instruction values into the code memory based on a menu type of arrangement.

3. The final screen display would display all the registers involved in executing a single instruction. The registers displayed would include the MAB, MBR, IR, program counter etc. This screen will allow the user to step through the whole cyle from loading PC into the MAB to the exectution of the decoded instruction.

In all software design it is necessary to describe the agorithm that is used to implement the coding. An example of the basic algorithm for interaction with the user is as follows.

```
START
Repeat for all code memory locations.
Ask user for opcode type
Read opcode type and convert opcode into a decimal value (see
above for values)
Instruction value equals operator.
Ask user for mode of opeartion (Direct/Indirect)
Read mode and convert mode into a decimal value
Instruction value equals instruction value + mode value
Ask user for operand value.
Instruction value equals instruction value + operand value.
Store instruction value into code memory location.
END
```

Once the user selects instructions to perform these are processed in accordance with the system algorithm an example of which is as follows,

```
START
Load PC count into the MAB
Fetch contents of memory location pointed to by MAB and place in the MBR.
Decode the instruction value in the MBR and place the opcode into the IR
IF mode is direct THEN
  Decode operand and place in the MBR
ELSE
  Decode the operand and place in the MAR

IF mode is direct THEN
  Execute instruction in the IR
ELSE
  Fetch contents of data location pointed to by MAB and place in the MBR

IF mode is direct THEN
  Increment the PC
ELSE
  Execute the instruction in the IR
```

These algorithms are used as the basis for coding the program, which is written in the C language and broken down into smaller functions. The decoding of an instruction can be achieved by using a mask to identify of the bits of an instruction byte that are relevant. By logically ANDing the mask with the instruction value any mask bits that are set to one will remain the same and any bit of the mask set to zero will make the corresponding bits of the instruction value zero.

Simulator Code in C

An example C program that can implement the simulator is given next. This is a very simple program that is used simply to illustrate how a simulator can be implemented.

```c
/* THE SIMULATION OF 8 BIT CPU */
#include <stdio.h>

#define LDA 0              /*instruction definitions*/
#define STA 1
#define ADD 2
#define BRA 3
#define BEQ 4
#define STOP 8
void display_setbits(unsigned);   /*declaration of function prototype*/
void main(void)             /*starting function main*/
{
unsigned int PC;          /*declaration of registers*/
unsigned int D0 = 0x00;
unsigned  int MAR;
unsigned int MBR;
unsigned int IR;
unsigned int Operand;
unsigned int SOURCE;
unsigned int Opcode;
unsigned int AMODE;
unsigned int MEMORY[16];
unsigned int RUN;
printf("enter starting address in hex....");    /*get the starting address*/
scanf("%u", &PC);
printf("enter '1' to Run '0' to stop\n");       /*get command to run or stop*/
scanf("%u\n", &RUN);
 while (RUN)                          /*starting of CPU operations*/
   {
   MAR=PC;
    PC=PC+1;
   (MBR=MEMORY[MAR]);
   printf("MBR = ");
    display_setbits(MBR);
     IR=MBR;
 Opcode = IR>>5;
 AMODE=(IR & 0X10) >> 4;
 Operand=IR & 0X0F;
 printf("%u\n", &Operand);
 if ( AMODE==0) SOURCE=MEMORY[Operand];    /*decode the address mode*/
 else SOURCE=Operand;
 switch (Opcode)                 /*decode the Opcode*/
 { case LDA:{D0=SOURCE; break;}
  case STA:{MEMORY[Operand]= 0; break;}
  case ADD:{D0=D0+SOURCE; break;}
  case BRA:{PC=Operand; break;}
```

```
    case BEQ:{if (D0==0) PC=Operand; break;}
    case STOP:{RUN=0; break;}
    }
    printf("Operand is.. ");              /*output the Operand*/
    display_setbits(Operand);

    printf("Opcode is..  ");
    display_setbits(Opcode);              /*output the Opcode value*/

    printf("The AMODE is...");
    display_setbits(AMODE);
    printf("enter '1' to RUN '0' to stop\n");
    scanf("%u\n", &RUN);
    }
    }
    void display_setbits(unsigned value)       /*function to convert and display the binary value*/
    {
    unsigned a, displaybits = 1 << 15;
    printf("%7u = ", value);
    for (a = 1; a <= 16; a++)
    {
    putchar(value & displaybits ? '1' : '0');
    value <<= 1;
    if (a % 8 == 0)                  /*put a space after 8 bits*/
    putchar(' ');
    }
    putchar('\n');
    }
```

The code listing shows the initial declaration of instructions identified earlier. (i.e.)

```
#define LDA 0         /*instruction definitions*/
#define STA 1
#define ADD 2
#define BRA 3
#define BEQ 4
#define STOP 8
```

The registers that we are using are also declared (i.e.)

```
unsigned int PC;        /*declaration of registers*/
unsigned int D0 = 0x00;
unsigned  int MAR;
unsigned int MBR;
unsigned int IR;
unsigned int Operand;
unsigned int SOURCE;
unsigned int Opcode;
unsigned int AMODE;
unsigned int MEMORY[16];
unsigned int RUN;
```

The program identifies the bits that are set in a byte by using the set bit function to isolate individual bits in a byte. (i.e.)

```
void display_setbits(unsigned);    /*declaration of function prototype*/
```

This function is declared as a prototype at the beginning. It is a requirement in C programming that you must declare all functions before you use them. The actual code for this function is listed at the end of the program. (i.e.)

```
void display_setbits(unsigned value)      /*function to convert and display the binary value*/
{
unsigned a, displaybits = 1 << 15;
printf("%7u = ", value);
for (a = 1; a <= 16; a++)
{
putchar(value & displaybits ? '1' : '0');
value <<= 1;
if (a % 8 == 0)                  /*put a space after 8 bits*/
putchar(' ');
}
putchar('\n');
}
```

The operation of this function is fairly self-explanatory and it is scanning through the byte to identify, which bits are 1 and which are 0.

The main body of the programme performs an infinite loop using the WHILE command. The sequence of operation which is repeated is to load the memory address register (MAR) with the current value of the PC register, the PC is incremented to point to the next instruction, and contents of MAR placed into the buffer register (MBR). There follow commands to display values on the screen, and then the value of MBR is placed in the instruction register (IR). At this point we have the 8-bit code that represents the full instruction in the IR. (i.e.) The function to display these is then called.

```
while (RUN)                    /*starting of CPU operations*/
{
 MAR=PC;
 PC=PC+1;
 (MBR=MEMORY[MAR]);
 printf("MBR = ");
 display_setbits(MBR);
 IR=MBR;
```

The bits are allocated according to our design, so that the 3 left-most bits are the Opcode, the 4 right-most bits the Operand and the 4th bit from the left the addressing mode. In order that we may identify each of these the programme implements masking using the AND function. (i.e.)

```
Opcode = IR>>5;
AMODE=(IR & 0X10) >> 4;
Operand=IR & 0X0F;
printf("%u\n", &Operand);
```

The selection of the instruction is obtained using the case statement, which take the result of the logical ANDing and use this to go through a set of cases, each of which represents and instruction. When the case matches the instruction the switch loop breaks and the instruction is processed. (i.e.)

```
if ( AMODE==0) SOURCE=MEMORY[Operand];   /*decode the address mode*/
else SOURCE=Operand;
 switch (Opcode)                /*decode the Opcode*/
{ case LDA:{D0=SOURCE; break;}
  case STA:{MEMORY[Operand]= 0; break;}
  case ADD:{D0=D0+SOURCE; break;}
  case BRA:{PC=Operand; break;}
  case BEQ:{if (D0==0) PC=Operand; break;}
  case STOP:{RUN=0; break;}
  }
```

The selecting 1 to run or 0 to stop controls this programme. The above programme and the brief explanation should be sufficient to describe the basic operation of a CPU. It is left to the reader to survey literature and find more detailed description if required.

Exercises

5.1.   Discuss the 4 main components that have to be included in the instruction set

5.2.   Discuss and provide examples of the 5 types of instructions that are typically supported in CPU design.

5.3.   Instructions work on Operands. Discuss how the CPU can be designed to process the addressing of Operands.

5.4.   Explain the basic operation of the CPU in relation to the execution of a programme in memory. Include in your answer typical sequence of operations that have to be performed and how the internal registers are affected.

5.5.   A CPU receives a sequence of two bytes to execute, namely B0 A2. Which of these bytes contains the Opcode?

5.6.   In a programming context describe the levels of programming and how they relate to accessing the CPU. Are there any parts of the CPU that are not accessible to programmers? If so why not?

5.7.   What is register transfer language used for?

5.8. Using RTL notation describe the programme to calculate the area of a triangle.

5.9. Describe the internal structure of a typical CPU. Include in your description the typical registers that need to be present, and discuss why this is so?

5.10. The CPU registers are made up of a number of flip-flops connected in an arrangement that enables bits to be transferred between them. Describe how D-Type flip-flops can be used to transfer bits between registers. In your answer include typical timing waveforms that can be expected during transfer of bits.

5.11. Figure ex.11 shows the internal structure of a CPU. The various registers are shown interconnected and a number of gates are used to control the flow of bits between these. Using RTL notation as necessary, explain how this diagram relates to the processing of an instruction such as ADD [Address], Data Register.

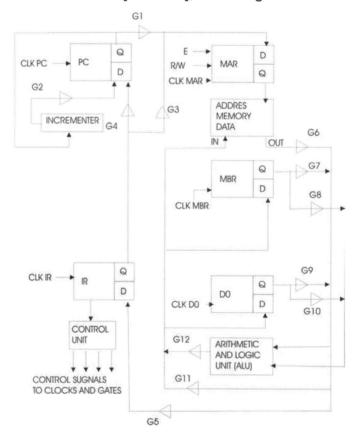

5.12. Figure Ex 11

5.13. For the situation in Q11 above, discuss the significance of the microprogramme in relation to the diagram and the execution of instructions. List the microinstructions that are required to perform the operation.

5.14. What is the purpose of the control unit and what are its basic components?

5.15. What are the main features to be considered in design of the instruction set for a CPU?

5.16. Table Q15 shows an instruction set for an 8-bit CPU. The CPU has been designed according to the following bit fields.

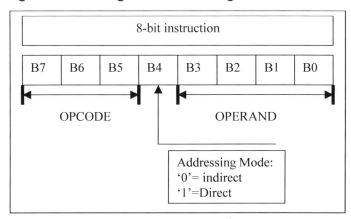

Table Q15. Initial instruction set (direct addressing)

Value	Instruction	Mnemonic	RTL description
00000000	Load accumulator with operand	LDA Dir N	[A]<N
00100000	Store Acc in data memory location	STORE Dir N	[M(N)]<[A]
01000000	Add data contents to Acc	ADD Dir N	[A]<[A]+N
01100000	Branch to prog memory location	BRA Dir N	[PC]<N
10000000	Compare accumulator with data and branch to prog memory location if the valuses are equal	BEQ Dir N	[A]=N?,[PC]<N
11100000	Stop execution	STOP	[PC]<STOP
00010000	Load accumulator with operand from memory location N	LDA InDir [N]	[A]<[N]
01010000	Add data contents of memory location N to Acc	ADD InDir N	[A]<[A]+[N]

5.17. For this arrangement consider the following byte sequence that constitute a simple program that needs to be executed on this CPU. Describe each instruction in RTL and show how any registers or memory locations are affected as each instruction executes.

The sequence of bytes to execute is: 00 02 40 04 20 08 50 08 F0

136

5.18. You are required to design the architecture for an 8-bit CPU, which will be used to control a robotic manipulator. The position of the manipulator is controlled by 8-bit signals sent to the manipulator buffer register. To obtain the current position the CPU takes binary inputs via its I/O ports. In order to describe the control the CPU must apply Boolean logic analysis on all inputs. The primary logic circuits that are needed are the AND, OR, NOT and XOR gates. Making any assumptions that you consider appropriate design the instruction set for this CPU.

CHAPTER 6 PIPELINING

6.1   Introduction

Pipelining is a method of arranging tasks in a special way so that, as a group they can be executed more efficiently. Consider for example that all instructions follow the FETCH-EXECUTE cycle described earlier. This means that at any one time the CPU is either fetching or executing, but it cannot do both at the same time. If a CPU is designed so that separate hardware is used for fetching then it should be possible for the CPU to be executing at the same time as fetching is being performed. This arrangement was used in the design of the Intel 8088 CPU, where the bus interface unit (BIU) was doing the fetching while the execution unit (EU) performed the execution of instructions. In other words while the EU is executing an instruction the BIU is fetching the next instruction. Since the EU and BIU perform different tasks, there is an instruction queue (or pipeline) where the BIU places instructions in the order that they should be executed. For example, the 8086 could store up to 6 instructions in this queue. The IA-32 (Intel Architecture, 32-bit) is a 32-bit extension of the original Intel x86 processor architecture. Even though the instruction set has remained intact, the successive generations of microprocessors that run it have become much faster. Before describing the evolution of pipelining we need to consider briefly the processing of an instruction.

Execution of an instruction

As mentioned in Chapter 5 of this text, a microprocessor needs to be told what to do and providing it with a sequence of instructions in the form of a programme does this. The execution of an instruction is done in a sequence of three steps,

1.   Fetch
2.   Decode
3.   Execute

This should make sense since the instruction resides in memory and needs to be fetched first. When it is fetched it has to be put somewhere so that it can be decoded. After it is fetched the instruction is stored as a bit pattern in a special register called the instruction register (IR) inside the control unit. Before this instruction can be executed it needs to be decoded by a decoder, which is also inside the control unit. The control unit then generates the appropriate signals and the instruction is executed. (See Chapter 5 of this text)

An instruction can be longer than 8-bits and can be formed of two or more words. The first word of the instruction contains the operation code (Opcode). By decoding this Opcode the microprocessor will know whether it needs to fetch more information from memory in order to execute the instruction. The control unit looks after the complete fetch-decode-execute process.

6.2 CISC and RISC Processors

The first computers that came into general use had very simple set of instructions which included add, subtract, increment, decrement, shift left and right etc. (i.e. Intel 8080). Later version such as the Intel 8088 had more complex instructions to include multiply, divide, decimal adjust etc.

As the instruction set became more complex these computers became known as CISC (Complex Instruction Set Computers) and they were the first type of personal computers (PCs). Every CISC instruction in a programme was decoded by the control unit and executed by the CPU.

At some stage in development, computer designers considered the idea of reducing the instruction set to a set of primitives and arranging a number of these to work in parallel. These were called Reduced Instruction Set Computers (RISC). In this way the instructions were made simple and they executed quickly. Provided that a large number of CPUs were available to execute instructions in parallel the result would provide fast computational speeds.

Consider for example the multiplication of two integers. i.e. $5 \times 4 = 20$. Assume that the instruction to ADD two numbers takes 10 CPU clock cycles to execute. If the multiplication instruction is not supported in the CPU instruction set, any multiplication can be performed by repetitive addition. For example to multiply 5×4 starting from result=0, perform addition of 5 to the result, four times. Each addition takes 10 clocks and so after four of these the time taken to execute the sum is 40 clocks. This is shown in Table 6.1.

Table 6.1

Clocks	0	10	10	10	10
Instruction	-	ADD 5	ADD 5	ADD 5	ADD 5
Result	0	5	10	15	20

Thus, ignoring any time lost to for example, jumps in a software loop, the multiplication takes 40 clock cycles to complete. If on the other hand four separate processors were used in parallel to execute the same arithmetic, then each would perform the addition in 10 clocks. Consequently, and assuming that data dependencies are neglected the multiplication instruction could complete in approximately 10 clock cycles, which is four times faster. (See Figure 6.1).

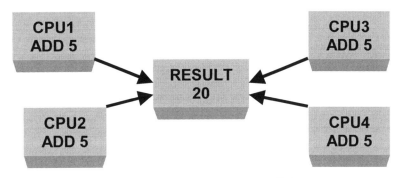

Figure 6.1. RISC execution by parallel processors

140

As a brief comparison, Table 6.2 shows some general features of CISC and RISC.

Table 6.2 CISC and RISC features for comparison

CISC Advantages	CISC Disadvantages
Instructions are closer to a high-level language (HLL) and therefore easier to understand and program	Many different instruction codes with complex addressing modes. Difficult to program at low level.
Programming more compact	Variable length of instructions making the time of execution difficult to predict.
Faster and more elegant writing of the application	Non-standard instruction structure (i.e. complex) does not provide for fast execution
Complexity in the instruction set can reduce memory requirements of executing programmes and so execution requires fewer bytes.	
RISC characteristics	
Simple instruction set	
Clear separation between instructions	
Standard instructions, bytes and execution time	
Unit of decoding can be hardwired (i.e. not micro coded) providing faster execution	
Large number of general purpose registers	
As computers evolved, changes were in the favour of RISC. These included the following improvements, Caches to speed instruction fetches. Large increases in RAM memory chips and price reduction. Better pipelining. Advanced optimising compilers.	

6.3   Pipelining

As mentioned earlier, all computers follow the basic fetch-execute cycle in order to process the instructions of a computer program. It makes sense, because it would be impossible to execute something that has not been made available, i.e. fetched. Pipelining refers to the principle of splitting the fetch-execute cycle of an instruction into smaller sections that can be processed independently. In this manner, a pre-processor can process a particular stage while at the same time the CPU can be executing another stage. Simply put, if there was one pre-processor doing the fetching, and the CPU doing the executing of instruction, the speed of processing the instruction would be significantly improved. As mentioned earlier the Intel 8086 family of processors, used the internal architecture which split the fetch and the execute stages between the bus interface unit (BIU) and the execution unit (EU). Typically in modern computer architectures, pipelines are split in the following stages, [25]

1.   Fetch instructions from memory.

2.   Read registers and decode the instruction.

3.   Execute the instruction or calculate an address.

4.   Access an operand in data memory.

5.   Write the result into a register.

Figure 6.2 shows how these stages could be organised within the CPU architecture. Here each of the 5 stages is uniquely identified and each instruction passes through a branch detector to decide if there are dependencies associated with that instruction. If there are no dependencies then the instruction can join the pipeline. On the other hand where an instruction has dependencies then it has to be executed when these have been resolved.

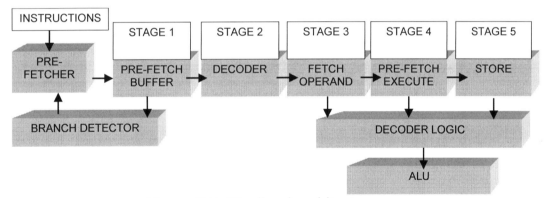

Figure 6.2. Pipelined architecture

Individual processing units can perform the 5 stages of processing, and so at any on time 5 separate instructions are being processed in a stage. For the pipeline stages shown in 6.3 to work, the various stages (1-5) need to complete in the same amount of time. Thus, the length of the longest stage determines the length of the pipeline. For this reason, CISC processors have difficulties with pipelining because of differing lengths of instructions. Pipelining is therefore more common with RISC processors where instruction set is reduced, and all instructions are of the same length. In an ideal situation, each stage in a RISC processor pipeline should complete in 1 clock cycle. This would mean that the processor finishes an instruction every clock cycle and averages one cycle per instruction (CPI).

Instruction 1	Stage 1	Stage 2	Stage 3	Stage 4	Stage 5
Instruction 2	Stage 2	Stage 3	Stage 4	Stage 5	Stage 1
Instruction 3	Stage 3	Stage 4	Stage 5	Stage 1	Stage 2
Instruction 4	Stage 4	Stage 5	Stage 1	Stage 2	Stage 3
Instruction 5	Stage 5	Stage 1	Stage 2	Stage 3	Stage 4
Time units	1	2	3	4	5

Figure 6.3. Simplified instruction pipelining stages

Figure 6.4 shows a simplified diagram of the Intel dual pipeline architecture as used in Pentium processors. [17] Here the control unit comprises two separate pipelines (U and V), which can process instructions in parallel. The pre-fetch buffers and instruction decode blocks are there to ensure that instruction level parallelism is possible. Parallelism here refers to the ability for instructions to execute in parallel. For example, when instructions of different lengths are being moved along several pipelines, each will complete at different times. On a CISC processor this will lead to instructions completing out of sequence. To some extent RISC avoids this by keeping instructions the same length and making it easier for instructions to be pipelined in parallel. This does not reduce the problem of procedural or data dependency, but it does at least mean that completion of instructions in parallel will not cause out of sequence execution. [26]

This instruction level parallelism that is supported by RISC processors is a very strong argument for their use. While CISC processors still exist, they are increasingly being improved to look more like RISC. [27]

143

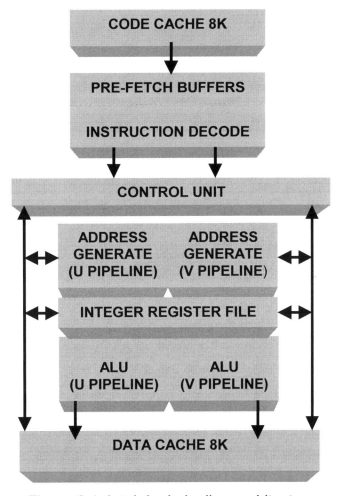

Figure 6.4. Intel dual pipeline architecture

6.4   Super-pipelining

Since pipelining refers to dividing the pipeline into steps then in theory, the more stages there are, the faster the pipeline will become because each stage can be performed at the same time as other stages for different instructions. Note that concurrent execution of a stage is not possible in pipelined architectures. This can only be done with scalar architectures, which will be discussed later in this chapter.

Thus in theory a pipeline with five stages should be five times faster than a non-pipelined processor. The instructions are executed after the 5 stages have been completed, but the pipelined architecture means that 5 separate instructions can be processed at the same time, each of these being in a different stage of the pipeline at any one unit of processing time. The speed at which each stage completes does not change but components of 5 different instructions are processed at each stage and therefore it appears as though each stage takes one fifth of the amount of time that the non-pipelined instruction takes. Thus the more pipelined stages we have the faster the execution of instructions. Some of the stages that can be included are as follows,

1. Instruction Fetch (First Half)
2. Instruction Fetch (Second Half)
3. Register Fetch
4. Instruction Execute
5. Data Cache Access (First Half)
6. Data Cache Access (Second Half)
7. Tag Check
8. Write Back

In this case we have 8-stage pipeline and every instruction can be in one of these stages at any one time. This is shown in Figure 6.5. This concept can be extended to as many pipeline stages, as it is possible to run independently. Note however that the list of stages above shows a single stage for the execute instruction. Since the CPU can only execute one instruction at any one time, this stage cannot be shared by any other instruction unless scalar architecture is employed. Other stages however that do no use the CPU can in some cases be performed at the same time.

This arrangement of tasks relies on the fact that an instruction can be processed in a number of independent stages. Provided that there is no dependency in the instruction then each stage can complete independently of other stages. Where this is possible, pipelining can significantly speed up the processing of instructions. An enhancement of basic pipelining is possible by refining the stages that constitute the pipeline. With more independent stages it is possible to process the instruction with a finer degree of granularity. This leads us to the concept of super-pipelining. The idea behind super pipelining is that pipelined stages can complete in less than one cycle. This can be achieved by providing finer granularity within the pipeline. In this manner more

145

instructions can exist in the pipeline and potentially this means that each pipelined stage can execute in less than one clock cycle.

Instruction 1	Stage 1	Stage 2	Stage 3	Stage 4	Stage 5	Stage 6	Stage 7	Stage 5
Instruction 2	Stage 2	Stage 3	Stage 4	Stage 5	Stage 6	Stage 7	Stage 8	Stage 1
Instruction 3	Stage 3	Stage 4	Stage 5	Stage 6	Stage 7	Stage 8	Stage 1	Stage 2
Instruction 4	Stage 4	Stage 5	Stage 6	Stage 7	Stage 8	Stage 1	Stage 2	Stage 3
Instruction 5	Stage 5	Stage 6	Stage 7	Stage 8	Stage 1	Stage 2	Stage 3	Stage 4
Instruction 6	Stage 6	Stage 7	Stage 8	Stage 1	Stage 2	Stage 5	Stage 1	Stage 2
Instruction 7	Stage 7	Stage 8	Stage 1	Stage 2	Stage 3	Stage 1	Stage 2	Stage 3
Instruction 8	Stage 8	Stage 1	Stage 2	Stage 3	Stage 4	Stage 2	Stage 3	Stage 4
Time units	1	2	3	4	5	6	7	8

Here each of the 8 instructions executes in 8 time units. Because of pipelining all 8 instructions can complete in 8 time units.
Without pipelining the 8 instruction would require 64 time units to complete.
With Super-pipelining (if each stage completes in half clock-cycle, the 8 instructions could complete in 4 time units.

Figure 6.5. Increasing the number of pipelined stages

For example consider the fetch cycle shown in Figure 6.6 where at the top it is shown that a single stage executes in one cycle. Consider now that this fetch was broken up into two smaller units fetch1 and fetch2 then each of these smaller units could complete in less than 1 cycle. Since two separate fetch stages exist, this means that two separate instructions can enter the stages. Thus it is seen that the fetch operation that takes 1 cycle to complete with one instruction, actually completes in less than one cycle when more instructions are able to enter the fetch1 and fetch2 stages. Or in other words, looking at the bottom diagram of Figure 6.6, a fetch stage is completed every half-cycle.

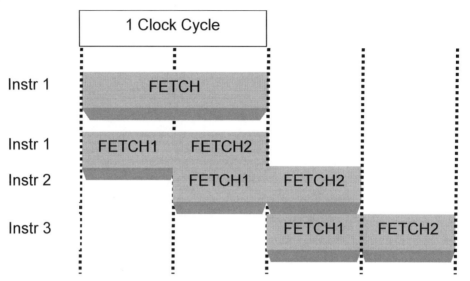

Figure 6.6. Refining granularity of a stage

Therefore if each stage discussed earlier in Figure 6.5 could execute in half a cycle, then in theory the 8 instructions could complete in 4 clocks. However, in practice, with far more instructions in a super-pipelined micro architecture, handling of events that disrupt the pipeline, such as cache misses, interrupts and branch mis-prediction, can be costly. [28]

6.5   Superscalar architectures

The term superscalar is used to describe CPUs, which are capable of performing more than one instruction per clock cycle. This is made possible by scaling the CPU design so that it consists of several independent decoders. This means that internal components of the processor are replicated so that it can process multiple instructions in the available pipeline stages. Thus, in theory parallel operation is possible in each of the pipelines. Furthermore, in order to improve performance, superscalar processors are designed to support instruction level parallelism, which refers to the extent to which instructions are able to execute in parallel. Thus a superscalar processor will fetch multiple instructions and then attempt to identify those that are independent of each other so that they can be executed in parallel. However, while in theory this should improve performance the question of dependence between instructions is an issue? For example, with a 5-stage pipeline, it is possible to have 5 separate instructions in the pipeline. With super scaling if two of these pipelines were used, then theoretically 10 instructions could be in the scaled pipelines. The chance that some of these instructions would depend on another in either of the pipelines becomes a strong possibility. In this situation the instruction cannot complete within the stage and the pipeline stalls. Table 6.3 shows the basic types of dependency between instructions.

Table 6.3 Various type of dependency between instructions

Dependency	Description	Example	Blocked until
Data	Read after write	MOV AL,05 ADD AL,10	AL is loaded
Procedural	The outcome of one instruction requires another instruction to complete	CMP AL,0F JZ Exit	Zero flag is set
Resource	Limited availability of a resource (i.e. FPU)	Floating-point Unit (FPU) in use	FPU Free

Other resource examples: memory, cache, registers, bus, ALU etc.

Dynamic pipelines

In order to reduce the impact of dependency dynamic pipelines are designed with the capability to schedule around stalls. Typically a dynamic pipeline comprises three units namely,

1. Instruction fetch and decode unit
2. A number of independent functional units, which reflect the number of stages in the pipeline. Each of these has a selection of buffers to temporarily store Opcodes and operands.

3. A commit unit that determines which instruction can proceed to the pipeline.

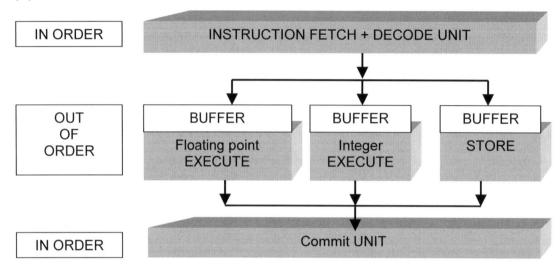

Figure 6.7. Dynamic pipelining

As seen in Figure 6.7 the different functional components are able to execute out-of-order and the buffers serve to store the results of these operations. The instruction decoder and the commit unit must execute in sequence. The idea behind dynamic pipelining is that when the instruction is executed and the result obtained, the commit unit decides when it is safe to proceed. If there is a dependency associated with the instruction then the processor can schedule other instructions to be executed until the stall is resolved. During this time the buffer stores the result and when the dependency is resolved it can proceed.

Performance comparison

In order to illustrate the principle of pipelining and scaling Figure 6.8 shows a comparison between the various approaches. If it is assumed that the 6 instructions in Figure 6.8 are not subject to any dependency then from the top of the figure the basic pipelined architecture shows that the 6 instructions can complete in 9 clock cycles (if it is further assumed that each stage requires one full clock cycle). By contrast, the super pipelined solution assumes that each stage can complete in half a clock cycle. The resulting performance is an improvement in speed so that all 6 instructions complete in 6.5 clock cycles. At the bottom of the figure a scaled architecture incorporating two separate pipelines shows a further improvement and the 6 instructions can complete in 6 clock cycles. Subject to dependency issues being resolved higher order of scaled pipelined stages are possible. However the issues arising from data, procedure and resource dependence are a major constraint.

INSTRUCTION	STAGE	1	2	3	4	1	2	3	4	1	
	CLOCKS	1	2	3	4	5	6	7	8	9	Basic pipeline (1 instruction per cycle). Although several instructions are in the pipeline only one is in the execute stage at any one time
	1	FETCH	DECODE	EXECUTE	WRITE						
	2		FETCH	DECODE	EXECUTE	WRITE					
	3			FETCH	DECODE	EXECUTE	WRITE				
	4				FETCH	DECODE	EXECUTE	WRITE			
	5					FETCH	DECODE	EXECUTE	WRITE		
	6						FETCH	DECODE	EXECUTE	WRITE	
	1	FETCH	DECODE	EXECUTE	WRITE						Super pipeline (1 instruction per half-cycle 2-pipelined stages are completed in every cycle
	2	FETCH	DECODE	EXECUTE	WRITE						
	3	FETCH	DECODE	EXECUTE	WRITE						
	4	FETCH	DECODE	EXECUTE	WRITE						
	5	FETCH	DECODE	EXECUTE	WRITE						
	6	FETCH	DECODE	EXECUTE	WRITE						
	1	FETCH	DECODE	EXECUTE	WRITE						Super-scaler pipeline (2 stages per cycle). Capable of executing two stages in parallel. Higher degree of scaling possible but subject to dependency
	2	FETCH	DECODE	EXECUTE	WRITE						
	3		FETCH	DECODE	EXECUTE	WRITE					
	4		FETCH	DECODE	EXECUTE	WRITE					
	5			FETCH	DECODE	EXECUTE	WRITE				
	6			FETCH	DECODE	EXECUTE	WRITE				

Figure 6.8. Comparison between the pipelined and scalar approaches

6.6   World's most powerful computers

Website at URL http://top500.org/ provides a list of the current state of the art in supercomputing. As at November 2008 the word's most powerful computer is the   Roadrunner   -   BladeCenter   QS22/LS21   Cluster, PowerXCell 8i 3.2 GHz / Opteron DC 1.8 GHz, Voltaire Infiniband. The basic characteristics are listed below (copied form the website)

System Name	**Roadrunner**
Site	DOE/NNSA/LANL
System Family	IBM Cluster
System Model	BladeCenter QS22 Cluster
Computer	BladeCenter QS22/LS21 Cluster, PowerXCell 8i 3.2 Ghz / Opteron DC 1.8 GHz , Voltaire Infiniband
Vendor	IBM
Application area	Not Specified
Installation Year	2008
Operating System	Linux
Interconnect	Infiniband
Processor	PowerXCell 8i 3200 MHz (12.8 GFlops)

Roadrunner, a new hybrid supercomputer, uses a video game chip to propel performance to petaflop/s speeds capable of more than a thousand trillion calculations per second. It is a cluster of approximately 3,250 compute nodes interconnected by an off-the-shelf parallel-computing network. Each compute node consists of two AMD Opteron dual-core microprocessors, with each of the Opteron cores internally attached to one of four enhanced Cell microprocessors. This enhanced Cell does double-precision arithmetic faster and can access more memory than the original Cell in a PlayStation 3. The entire machine will have almost 13,000 Cells and half as many dual-core Opterons.

Modern supercomputers have thousands of identical computer nodes, each containing a microprocessor and a separate memory. The nodes are connected to form a cluster and work simultaneously on a single problem. A huge obstacle to increased performance is the memory barrier. In the not-too-distant past, the time to fetch data from the node memory and load it into the processing units (called the "compute core") of a microprocessor was comparable to the time it would take that core to do the number crunching. Now the number crunching is 50 times faster than the time to fetch and load data. As a result the time spent in data retrieval and communications can no longer be ignored and the old solution for increasing supercomputer performance—miniaturising circuits and using faster clocks—is breaking down.

"We replace our high-performance supercomputers every four or five years," says Andy White, leader of supercomputer development at Los Alamos. "They become outdated in terms of speed, and the maintenance costs and failure rates get too high."

Exercises

6.1. Distinguish between RISC and CISC architectures. What are their respective advantages and disadvantages?

6.2. Discuss the trends in RISC architectures and their applications.

6.3. Explain the basic principle of pipelining, its benefits and limitations.

6.4. How does super-pipelining improve performance?

6.5. What is the basic principle of super-scalar architectures?

6.6. How does instruction dependence affect pipelined and scaled architectures?

6.7. What is dynamic pipelining, and how is it usually implemented.

6.8. Assuming that there is no dependency explain how the pipelined, super-pipelined and superscalar architectures compare in execution speeds.

CHAPTER 7 PARALLEL COMPUTING

7.1. Introduction

As processor speeds increase we are reaching a point where conventional communication speeds are approaching their physical limits. If you consider that all digital signals travel at the speed of light then you can relate the clock frequencies to the speed of signals travelling along buses. If the current CPUs run at 3GHz (i.e. $3 \times 10^9 Hz$) then the time for one full cycle is $\frac{1}{3 \times 10^9} Hz$. If it is assumed that electromagnetic signals travel at the speed of light then in this time they will cover a distance of:

$$ speed \times time = \frac{3 \times 10^8}{3 \times 10^9} = 0.1m = 10cm. $$

Since signals cannot travel faster than the speed of light then at this frequency the maximum distance that can be covered is 10cm. This means that if a bus within a CPU was longer than 10cm then signals could not reach between ends of the CPU within one cycle. Thus increasing processor and bus speeds alone will encounter physical limits before long and new ways of improving performance are necessary.

Recent trends have cantered on parallel computers, which can implement many independent operations simultaneously. The number of operations, which can be performed simultaneously, depends on the number of processors in the machine as well as its architecture.

7.2. Parallel computing

Traditionally programs were written to run as a sequence of instructions on a microprocessor with Von Neumann architecture. This architecture uses the stored-program concept. The CPU executes a stored program by performing read and write operations on the memory. With the improved manufacturing techniques and reduced cost of producing CPUs, parallel processing has became a viable option. Parallel computing attempts to perform more than a single operation at the same time. Initially multiprocessing solutions were implemented where a number of CPUs with Von Neumann architecture were arranged in a multiprocessing configuration. Further developments led to the design of dedicated processors that departed from the Von Neumann architecture and drifted towards parallel processing. Since the advent of parallel CPUs programming paradigms have developed to take advantage of these new architectures. Flynn's taxonomy distinguishes multi-processor computer architectures according to how they treat instructions and data. [29]

The four classifications defined by Flynn are based upon the number of concurrent instruction and data streams available in the architecture. Both the instruction stream and the data stream can be single or multiple, and this provides four basic categories, as shown in Figure 7.1.

SISD	SIMD
Single Instruction, Single Data	Single Instruction, Multiple Data
MISD	MIMD
Multiple Instruction, Single Data	Multiple Instruction, Multiple Data

Figure 7.1. Flynn's taxonomy

All programs need to access data from memory and there are a number of ways that this can be organised. From Flynn's taxonomy it should be relatively intuitive that the different categories will approach memory access in a different way. For example where multiple data is operated on there must be a different approach to memory access from when a single data stream is accessed. Figure 7.2 shows a summary of the types of memory and processor organisation in the four categories as described by Flynn. Although the figure contains much information it is intended to serve as a summary of the important features of each category. Memory access is crucial with multiple data streams and in the two categories (SIMD, MIMD) memory is either shared or distributed. MIMD is the most challenging category to implement because multiple instructions are accessing multiple data at the same time. As a result the organisation of memory and instruction streams offers a range of

154

possibilities. Memory can be shared in these systems in which case they are closely coupled so that read/write actions are controlled. This is further grouped into symmetric multiprocessing (SMP) and non-uniform memory access (NUMA). In loosely coupled system memory is distributed and this allows for clustering. [23] The various categories are briefly described next.

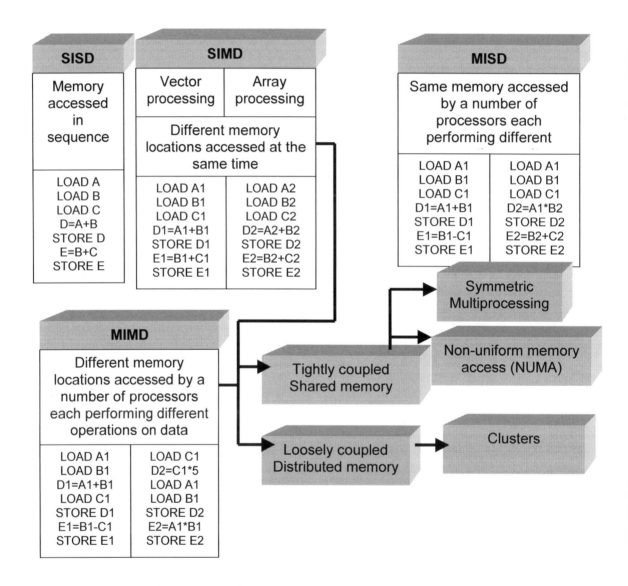

Figure 7.2. Memory options for different categories.

Single Instruction, Single Data stream (SISD)

This arrangement is a sequential computer, which does not exploit parallelism in either the instruction or data streams and therefore it, is not a parallel architecture. As seen in Figure 7.3 only one instruction stream (IS) is being acted on by the processing unit (PU) during any one-clock cycle. Also a single data stream (DS) is used from the memory unit (MU) during any one-clock cycle. Examples of SISD architecture are the traditional single processor architectures used in PCs or old mainframes.

SISD (Normal computer)

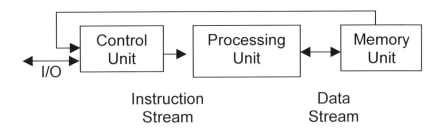

Figure 7.3. Basic characteristics of SISD.

Single Instruction, Multiple Data streams (SIMD)

This architecture exploits multiple data streams while using a single instruction stream to perform operations, which may be executed in parallel. An example of this configuration is an array processor (also called vector processor). Thus a large data stream is operated on by a single instruction. Figure 7.4 shows the basic operation of this type of processor. It is a parallel architecture where all processing units execute the same instruction at any given clock cycle. The instruction is fed though the CU to a number of PUs and each of these can operate on a different data element (LM_n).

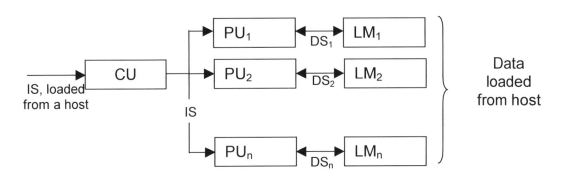

Figure 7.4. SIMD Architecture

SIMD architectures are very popular because of their ability to manipulate large vectors and matrices in minimum time. This finds particular use in such areas as weather data and cancer radiation research. By definition, a vector processor, or array processor, is a CPU design that is able to run mathematical operations on multiple data elements simultaneously. This is in contrast to a scalar processor, which handles one element at a time. The vast majority of present days CPUs are scalar. Vector processors were common in the scientific computing area, where they formed the basis of most supercomputers through the 1980s and into the 1990s, but general improvements in performance and processor design saw the near disappearance of the vector processor as a general-purpose CPU. [30]

The power behind this type of architecture can be seen when the number of processor elements is equivalent to the size of the vector. In this situation, addition and multiplication of vector elements can be done simultaneously. Even when the size of the vector is larger than the number of processors elements available, the speedup, compared to a sequential algorithm, is immense. There are two types of SIMD architectures the True SIMD and the Pipelined SIMD. Each has its own advantages and disadvantages but their common attribute is superior ability to manipulate vectors. [31] A brief description is given next.

True SIMD: Distributed Memory

True SIMD architecture contains a single CU with multiple PUs as shown in Figure 7.4. In this situation, the PUs act as slaves to the CU. They cannot fetch or interpret any instructions. In other words they are merely a unit, which has capabilities of addition, subtraction, multiplication, and division. Each PU has access only to its own memory. In this sense, if a PU needs the information contained in a different PU, it must put in a request to the CU and the CU must manage the transferring of information. The advantage of this type of architecture is in the relative ease of adding more memory and PU's to the computer. The disadvantage can be found in the time wasted by the CU managing all the memory exchanges.

True SIMD: Shared Memory

Another true SIMD architecture is designed with a configurable association between the PU's and the memory units (MUs). In this architecture, memory units replace the local memories that were attached to each PU as described earlier. All the PU's through an alignment network or switching unit share these MUs. This allows for the individual PU's to share their memory without accessing the CU. This type of architecture is superior to the distributed memory architecture described above, but a disadvantage is inherited in the difficulty of adding memory.

Pipelined SIMD

Pipelined SIMD architecture is composed of a pipeline of PUs with shared memory. The pipeline takes different streams of instructions and performs all the operations of a PU. The pipeline is a first in first out (FIFO) arrangement. To take advantage of the pipeline, the data to be evaluated must be stored in different MUs so that the pipeline can be supplied with this information as fast as possible. The advantages of this architecture can be found in the speed and efficiency of data processing.

Multiple Instruction, Single Data stream (MISD)

In this configuration multiple instructions operate on a single data stream. This type of architecture is rarely implemented and is generally used only for fault tolerance. Heterogeneous systems operate on the same data stream and must agree on the result. Examples include the Space Shuttle flight control computer. [29] Figure 7.5 shows the operation of MISD architecture. Here it is seen that a single data stream is fed into multiple processing units. Each PU operates on the data independently via independent instruction streams (ISs).

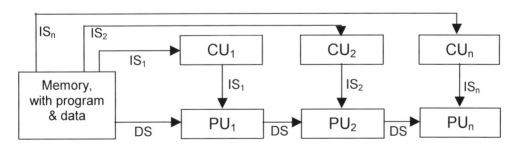

Figure 7.5. MISD Architecture

Multiple Instruction, Multiple Data streams (MIMD)

Machines using MIMD have a number of processors that function asynchronously and independently. At any time, different processors may be executing different instructions on different pieces of data. MIMD architectures may be used in a number of application areas such as computer-aided design/computer-aided manufacturing, simulation, modelling, and as communication switches. MIMD machines can be of either shared memory or distributed memory categories. These classifications are based on how MIMD processors access memory. Shared memory machines may be of the bus-based, extended, or hierarchical type. Distributed memory machines may have hypercube or mesh interconnection schemes. In this architecture multiple autonomous processors are simultaneously executing different instructions on different data. Distributed systems are generally recognised to be MIMD architectures, either exploiting a single shared memory space or a distributed memory space. Figure 7.6 shows the basic architecture of MIMD processors.

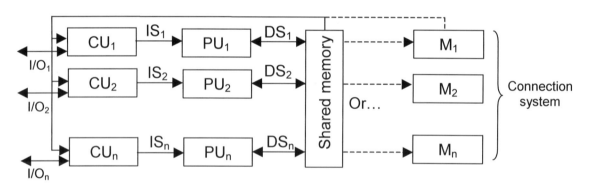

Figure 7.6. MIMD architecture

As seen in Figure 7.6 MIMD architectures have a number of independent PUs so that at any time, different PUs may be executing different instructions on different pieces of data. MIMD architectures may be used in a number of application areas such as computer-aided design/computer-aided manufacturing, simulation, and as communication switches. MIMD machines can be of either shared memory or distributed memory categories. These classifications are based on how MIMD processors access memory. Shared memory machines may be bus-based, extended, or hierarchical type.

Distributed memory machines may have hypercube or mesh interconnection schemes. [31]

Shared Memory: Bus-based (MIMD)

MIMD machines with shared memory have processors, which share a common, central memory. In the simplest form, all processors are attached to a bus, which connects them to memory. This is called bus-based shared memory. Bus-based machines may have another bus that enables them to communicate directly with each another. This additional bus is used for synchronisation among the processors. When using bus-based shared memory MIMD machines, only a small number of processors can be supported. There is contention among the processors for access to shared memory, and these machines are limited for this reason. These machines may be incrementally expanded up to the point where there is too much contention on the bus.

Shared Memory: Extended (MIMD)

MIMD machines with extended shared memory attempt to avoid or reduce the contention among processors for shared memory by subdividing the memory into a number of independent memory units. These memory units are connected to the processors by an interconnection network. The memory units are treated as a unified central memory. One type of interconnection network for this type of architecture is a crossbar-switching network. In this type of network, a crossbar switch is a device that is capable of channelling data between any two devices that are attached to it, up to its maximum number of ports. The paths set up between devices can be fixed for some duration or changed when desired and each device-to-device path (going through the switch) is usually fixed for some period. Crossbar topology can be contrasted with bus topology, an arrangement in which there is only one path that all devices share. Traditionally, computers have been connected to storage devices with a large bus. A major advantage of crossbar switching is that, as the traffic between any two devices increases, it does not affect traffic between other devices. In addition to offering more flexibility, a crossbar switch environment offers greater scalability than a bus environment. Thus, in this

160

scheme, N processors are linked to M memory units which requires N times M switches. However, this is not economically feasible for connecting a large number of processors due to the complex switching arrangement. [32]

Shared Memory: Hierarchical (MIMD)

MIMD machines with hierarchical shared memory use a hierarchy of buses to give processors access to each other's memory. Processors on different boards may communicate through internal buses that connect the nodes. With this type of architecture, the machine may support over a thousand processors. [31] There are a number of way to implement MIMD and these are briefly considered next.

Distributed Memory (MIMD):

In distributed memory MIMD machines, each processor has its own individual memory location. For data to be shared, it must be passed from one processor to another as a message. Since there is no shared memory, contention is not a major problem with these machines. However it is not economically feasible to connect a large number of processors directly to each other. A way to avoid this multitude of direct connections is to connect each processor to just a few others. This type of design can be inefficient because of the added time required to pass a message from one processor to another along the message path. The amount of time required for processors to perform simple message routing can be substantial. Systems were designed to reduce this time loss and hypercube and mesh configurations are two of the popular interconnection schemes. Some of these are briefly mentioned next. [31]

Fully connected memory (MIMD):

This is the most powerful interconnection network (topology): each node is directly connected to all other nodes. However as mentioned earlier it is not economically feasible to connect a large number of processors directly to each other. In this configuration each of the N nodes has N-1 connections as shown in Figure 7.7.

161

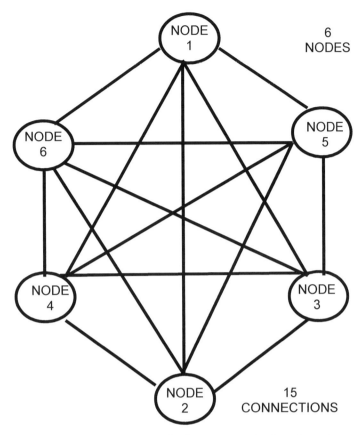

Figure 7.7. Fully connected network

Even though this is the best network to have the high number of connections per node mean that this network can only be implemented for small values of N. Therefore some form of limited interconnection network should be used.

Distributed Memory (MIMD): Hypercube Connection (Binary n-Cube)

Hypercube networks consist of $N=2^k$ nodes arranged in a k dimensional hypercube. The nodes are numbered $0,1, ...2^{k-1}$ and two nodes are connected if their binary labels differ by exactly one bit. An example is shown in Figure 7.8. Notice that nodes that connect to each other have a difference of a single bit value in binary. That is to say, node 00 connects to nodes 01 and 10 but NOT to node 11. Node 11 connects to nodes 01 and 10 but not to node 00. In this manner any node can only have two connections one to a node higher by 1 bit value and one to a node lower by 1 bit value.

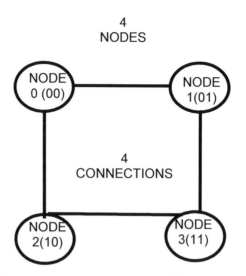

4
NODES

4
CONNECTIONS

Figure 7.8. Hypercube connections with 4 nodes (diameter 2)

In a MIMD distributed memory machine with a hypercube system interconnection network containing four processors, a processor and a memory module are placed at each vertex of a square. [33]

Combining two k-1 dimensional hypercubes and connecting the corresponding nodes forms a k-dimensional hypercube. Thus, each node is connected to k other nodes. The diameter of the system is the minimum number of steps it takes for one processor to send a message to the processor that is the farthest away. So, for example, in Figure 7.8 the diameter is 2, since this is the number of links needed to contact the most distant node. In a hypercube system with eight processors and each processor and memory module being placed in the vertex of a cube, the diameter is 3. This is shown in Figure 7.9.

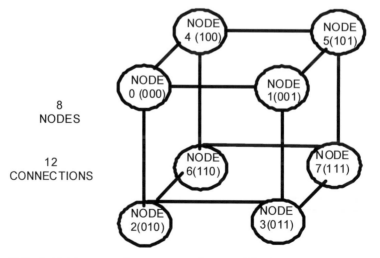

8
NODES

12
CONNECTIONS

Figure 7.9. 3-D Hypercube connections with 8 nodes (diameter 3)

In general, a system that contains 2^N processors with each processor directly connected to N other processors, the diameter of the system is N. One disadvantage of a hypercube system is that it must be configured in powers of two, so a machine must be built that could potentially have many more processors than is really needed for the application. [31] For example, N=3 uses 8 processor, the next level is N=4 which is 16 processors, and the next N=5 corresponds to 32 processors. The difference in the power of two means that a significantly larger number of processors are used after each increment in the power.

Distributed Memory (MIMD): Mesh Interconnection Network

In an MIMD distributed memory machine with a mesh interconnection network, processors are placed in a two-dimensional grid. This is shown in Figure 7.10 where it is seen that each processor is connected to its four immediate neighbours. Wraparound connections may be provided at the edges of the mesh. One advantage of the mesh interconnection network over the hypercube is that the mesh system does not need to be configured in powers of two. A disadvantage is that the diameter of the mesh network is greater than the hypercube for systems with more than four processors. [31]

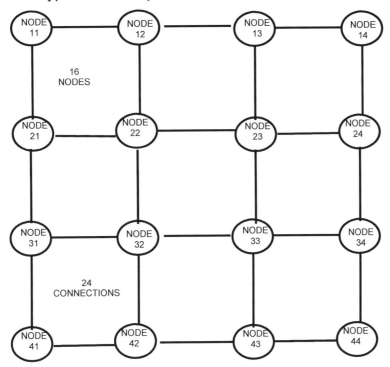

Figure 7.10. Mesh connected network

7.3. Multiprocessing with Closely Coupled Systems

These are bus-based systems that are connected by a back plane, enabling Uniform Memory Access (UMA) for fast inter process communication. [34] However with this arrangement there is a problem of bus overloading. To some extent the overloading is reduced with modern processors since they have their own caches, which minimise the use of the bus. However, this also has the side effect of introducing problems to do with cache/memory coherence problems. To mitigate this it becomes necessary to use write-back protocols (e.g. the MESI protocol used by Intel), which in turn cause additional load on the bus. Thus in reality bus based multiprocessing is very limited in the number of processes that it can support.

Single stage switched systems can support more processors - e.g. the crossbar system, with n^2 switches to connect any of n CPUs to any of n memory blocks. These are very fast, but very expensive in switches. Note that in electronics, a crossbar switch refers to a switch connecting multiple inputs to multiple outputs in a matrix manner.

Multistage switches, e.g. Omega hierarchical switched systems have fewer switches ($nlog_2n$) and are therefore cheaper, but they are slower because of delays across the switch banks. Also, since they have fewer switches, they cannot implement all the possible permutations as can the crossbar system. Large systems have been built, but expensively. Ultimately, multiprocessing is limited to fairly low numbers of CPUs. See the top 500 web site for details of very large multiprocessors, e.g. the Japanese 'Earth Simulator'. [35] For a system of n processors, and a bus width of w, the following table summarises the performance criteria.

	Bus based	Single-stage, e.g. crossbar	Multi-stage, e.g. Omega switched
Scalability, with n CPU's	Very limited, due to bus-bandwidth and cache coherence problems	Limited by cost, ~ n^2	Cost easier ~ $nlog_2n$ large systems have been built
Data transfer	UMA, constant	UMA, constant	Latency ~log n
Bandwidth	w/n	w to nw	w to nw
Switch complexity	order (n)	order (n*n)	order (log n)
Routing possibilities	1 to 1	All permutations, and broadcast	Limited permutations, including shuffle-exchange

From the aforementioned it can be said that single stage crossbars are faster and offer better performance, but at greatly increased cost, for larger systems.

7.4. Loosely Coupled Parallelism: Clusters

We have studied older architectures for loosely coupled parallelism, such as mesh and hypercubes, which require that special systems be built. This is also true for the switched, closely coupled architectures, such as crossbar systems, Omega switched networks etc. The major concern with special builds is the cost, which in practice is often not justified.

Rather than build expensive bespoke solutions an alternative is to take standard computers (e.g. Pentium PC's) and standard connections between them (e.g. Ethernet links or the Internet), connect them up and devise some suitable software to deliver parallel computing at much lower cost and potentially on a very big scale. Such systems were first set up in the 1990's (at NASA) and are now among the most important ways of achieving parallel processing power. They are called Clusters, or Clusters of Workstations (COWS)

Cluster basics

Clustering was covered earlier and it was suggested that it could be seen as the opposite of multitasking. This is not in a literal sense but rather as a concept. Clusters aim to apply a large number of processors to a single task, resulting in the task completing more quickly. Clusters can be 2 or more (even 1000's) of individual machines. They can be used for true parallel processing i.e. to apply more computing power to hard problems. Note that this is made more difficult since we need to devise distributed parallel algorithms to attack a problem at the many nodes of a cluster simultaneously. Consequently cluster solutions are largely problem specific, although groups of similar problems will have similar solutions.

Clusters are also used for 'load balancing', i.e. where a computer system has to service many largely independent jobs. In these applications we use the cluster to 'contract out' and divide up the jobs among the nodes of the cluster. Obviously, this is a way to set up powerful servers for large numbers of clients. This kind of load balancing is easier to implement than the 'single problem' applications mentioned in bespoke systems earlier, and it can be done with generic software tools.

Clusters provide very good scaling and fault tolerance. Since there is no special hardware and all the computers at every node are the exactly the same, nodes can be added to or removed from the cluster without problems – the only effect will be on the aggregate power available.

Small Clusters

The most common way to set these up is to use Linux, along with open source software such as Mosix and OSCAR, which allows PC clusters for load balancing to be set up in quite a straightforward manner.

These clusters can be used for true parallel processing i.e. to apply more computing power to hard problems. As mentioned earlier this is very difficult because we need to devise distributed parallel algorithms, which act at the many nodes of a cluster simultaneously. Consequently implementations of these clusters tend to be problem specific.

Big Clusters

Again, these are often based on Linux. The early NASA software was named 'Beowulf' and Beowulf systems are still being developed. The top 500 supercomputer web site (www.top500.org) from the University of Mannheim now lists Linux based clusters among the world's biggest, alongside the specially built giants from Cray, Silicon Graphics, IBM and Fujitsu (who built the Earth Simulator).

The SETI@Home (search for Extra terrestrial Intelligence) project is in effect a cluster of up to 3.5 million personal computers in 226 countries. A recent estimate of the aggregate PC time devoted in this way is 800,000 years!

Mosix

Mosix is the acronym for Multiple computer Operating System for Unix. It is used to extend the Linux kernel so that any standard Linux process can be migrated to another node so that it can take advantage of better resources or execute faster. The migrated process is not aware where it is and as far as its home node is concerned, the process is running locally. Migration can be automatic; each node is a master for locally created processes and a server for remote process that migrated from other nodes. There are monitoring algorithms showing what is going on where and how efficient everything is. But Mosix cannot run a single process on two or more nodes at the same time; consequently it comes into the 'load balancing' category.

OSCAR

Open Source Cluster Application Resource (OSCAR) consists of one server node and lots of clients, all of which must have the same hardware set-up. OSCAR provides an installation framework to install the necessary files and software resources among the clients. OSCAR is mostly aimed at High Performance Computing (HPC).

Beowulf

This is arguably the best-known Linux type cluster. Basically it provides multiple machine libraries of clustering tools. Perhaps the most interesting is the PVM (Parallel Virtual Machines) and MPI (Message Passing Interface). Both these allow for true parallel attack on difficult problems, but both need users who know how to write special software to hook into PVM or MPI in order to take advantage of the cluster. MPI in particular is a vendor independent standard for message passing, with a large user based applications forum.

Grids versus conventional supercomputers

"Distributed" or "grid" computing in general is a special type of parallel computing, which relies on complete computers (with onboard CPU, storage, power supply, network interface, etc.) connected to a network (private, public or the Internet) by a conventional network interface, such as Ethernet. This is in contrast to the traditional notion of a supercomputer, which has many processors connected by a local high-speed computer bus. [36]

7.5. Problems in Designing Parallel Algorithms

In order to be able to exploit parallel architectures, dedicated programming techniques must be implemented to facilitate parallel operation. Some of the issues in performing parallel operations are as follows,

1.   The number of processors, which can function in parallel.
2.   The size of the algorithm: which is the number of instructions that need to be executed in order to achieve the desired result.
3.   The depth of the algorithm, which refers to the number of operations in the longest chain of operations from any input to any output.

These are very closely related in that if for example there were an infinite number of processors to perform the algorithms, then computation time would be minimised if algorithms had minimum depth. That is to say there are sufficient parallel processors to implement all instructions in one cycle. The reverse is also true, so that if the number of processors is limited, then the depth of the algorithm should be increased in order to improve performance.

In reality design of modern systems is a compromise. As hardware advances enable more processors to be clustered so the algorithms that they need to execute reduce in depth. The evaluation of these algorithms focuses on speedup and efficiency. Speedup measures the increase or decrease of computational time of the parallel algorithm compared to a known sequential algorithm. Efficiency measures the increase or decrease of computational time per processor. [31]

7.6.   Parallel Programming Models

To exploit parallel hardware architectures the programmes that are designed to run on these must permit execution across a number of processors. Therefore the parallel programming models are an abstraction above hardware and memory architectures. Some of the common programming models in use are as follows,

- Shared Memory
- Threads

- Message Passing
- Data Parallel
- Hybrid

Shared Memory Model

In the shared-memory programming model, tasks share a common address space, which they read and write asynchronously. Potentially this could present a problem because a processor may modify memory before another processor has had access to it. To deal with this various mechanisms such as locks/semaphores may be used to control access to the shared memory.

An advantage of this model from the programmer's point of view is that the notion of data "ownership" is lacking, so that there is no need to explicitly specify the communication of data between tasks. Program development can often be simplified. An important disadvantage in terms of performance is that it becomes more difficult to understand and manage data locality.

Threads Model

In the threads model of parallel programming, a single process can have multiple concurrent execution paths. Each of these paths is a thread that can execute independently. Figure 7.11 shows how a program can be seen to consist of threads. Here the analogy that can be used to describe threads is the concept of a single program that includes a number of subroutines. From Figure 7.11 the following can be discerned,

- The main program a.out is scheduled to run by the operating system. It is loaded into memory and it acquires all of the necessary system and user resources to run.
- a.out performs some serial work, and then creates a number of tasks (threads) that can be scheduled and run by the operating system concurrently.
- Each thread has local data, but also, shares the entire resources of a.out. This saves the overhead associated with replicating a program's

resources for each thread. Each thread also benefits from a global memory view because it shares the memory space of a.out.

- A thread's work may best be described as a subroutine within the main program. Any thread can execute any subroutine at the same time as other threads.

- Threads communicate with each other through global memory (updating address locations). This requires synchronisation to insure that more than one thread is not updating the same global address at any time.

- Threads can come and go, but a.out remains present to provide the necessary shared resources until the application has completed.

- Threads are commonly associated with shared memory architectures and operating systems.

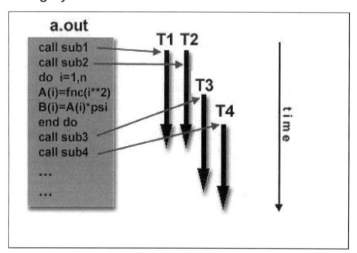

Figure 7.11. Basic principle of operation of the threads model. [36]

Message Passing Model

In this model parallel tasks communicate by passing messages. Typically messages include function invocation, signals, and data packets. The message-passing model demonstrates the following characteristics:

- A set of tasks that use their own local memory during computation. Multiple tasks can reside on the same physical machine as well as across an arbitrary number of machines.

- Tasks exchange data through communications by sending and receiving messages.

171

- Data transfer usually requires cooperative operations to be performed by each process. For example, a send operation must have a matching receive operation, as shown in Figure 7.12.

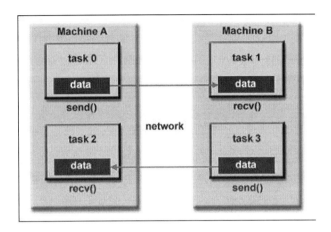

Figure 7.12. Message passing model

From a programming perspective, message-passing implementations commonly comprise a library of subroutines that are embedded in source code. The programmer is responsible for determining all parallelism.

Message Passing Interface (MPI) was released in 1994 and it is now the "de facto" industry standard for message passing. For shared memory architectures, MPI implementations usually do not use a network for task communications. Instead, they use shared memory (memory copies) for performance reasons.

Data Parallel Model

For many parallel computer applications, achieving good performance on a private memory requires exploiting data parallelism as well as task parallelism. Depending on the size of the input data set and the number of nodes (i.e., processors), different tradeoffs between task and data parallelism can be implemented. Most existing compilers focus on only one of either the data parallelism or task parallelism. Therefore, to achieve the desired results, the programmer must separately program and compile for the data and task parallelism. [37] The data parallel model demonstrates the following characteristics:

172

- Most of the parallel work focuses on performing operations on a data set. The data set is typically organised into a common structure, such as an array. This is depicted in Figure 7.13.
- A set of tasks work collectively on the same data structure, however, each task works on a different partition of the same data structure.
- Tasks perform the same operation on their partition of work, for example, "add 4 to every array element".
- On shared memory architectures, all tasks may have access to the data structure through global memory. On distributed memory architectures the data structure is split up and resides as "chunks" in the local memory of each task.

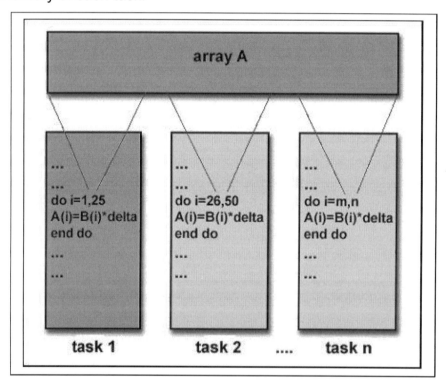

Figure 7.13. Data parallel model

Programming with the data parallel model is usually accomplished by writing a program with data parallel constructs. The constructs can be calls to a data parallel subroutine library or, compiler directives recognised by a data parallel compiler. Compiler Directives allow the programmer to specify the distribution and alignment of data. Fortran implementations are available for most common parallel platforms.

Distributed memory implementations of this model usually have the compiler convert the program into standard code with calls to a message passing library (MPI) to distribute the data to all the processes. All message passing is done invisibly to the programmer. [38]

Exercises

7.1. Describe Flynn's general classification of computer architectures. Using diagrams, or otherwise, explain how the instruction and data streams are handled in each of the four categories, which Flynn identifies. Indicate the relative importance of the different arrangements and briefly discuss types of application for which each of the architectures are suitable.

7.2. Explain what is meant by 'Multiprocessing with Closely Coupled Systems'.

7.3. Discuss the relative merits of mesh and hypercube arrangements for loosely coupled switched systems, explaining the concept of connection diameter and comparing the scaling properties of the two arrangements. Include a diagram of a 3-dimensional hypercube.

7.4. Briefly discuss the development of parallel multi-computers using clustering techniques, giving examples of current systems.

7.5. Given the definition: 'Clusters can be a minimum of 2 individual machines', describe the purpose of clusters and the difference between small and big clusters.

7.6. MIMD (Multiple Instruction Multiple Data stream) parallel architectures may be tightly coupled (multiprocessing) or loosely coupled (multicomputing). Outline the essential differences between these two approaches and give application examples of each.

7.7. In MIMD configuration compare and contrast the (bus, extended and hierarchical) shared memory models

7.8. Discuss the main problems encountered in the design of parallel algorithms.

7.9. Explain the main features of the following programming models,

      a)   Shared memory, b) Threads model

      c)   Message passing, d) Data parallel

References

Please note: All web pages accessed between June 2008 and January 2009.

Chapter 1
1. http://en.wikipedia.org/wiki/Computer_architecture
2. http://en.wikipedia.org/wiki/Comparison_of_operating_systems.
3. http://ieeexplore.ieee.org/xpl/freeabs_all.jsp?arnumber=1087187
4. SAP enterprise software, http://www.sap.com
5. Application programming definition, http://en.wikipedia.org/wiki/Application_programming
6. David Solomon, Mark Russinovich, Windows Internals and Advanced Troubleshooting Tutorial.
7. What Is the Definition of a TTL (Transistor-Transistor Logic) Compatible Signal? http://digital.ni.com/public.nsf/3efedde4322fef19862567740067f3cc/acb4bd7550c4374c86 256bfb0067a4bd
8. *Video RAM Technologies,* http://www.pcguide.com/ref/video/techVRAM-c.html

Chapter 2
9. Compute Cluster Network Requirements, Microsoft TechNet. http://technet2.microsoft.com/windowsserver/en/library/f49b19ee-aa05-4f16-8132-36ee09f631c11033.mspx?mfr=true
10. CNS 18 Technological impact of magnetic hard disk drives on storage systems by E. Grochowski and R. D. Halem, http://www.research.ibm.com/journal/sj/422/grochowski.html
11. Parallel computing, From Wikipedia, the free encyclopedia http://en.wikipedia.org/wiki/Parallel_computing.
12. B. B. Zhou, X. Qu and R. P. Brent, Effective Scheduling in a Mixed Parallel and Sequential Computing Environment, Computer Sciences Laboratory, The Australian National University, Canberra, ACT 0200, Australia wwwmaths.anu.edu.au/~brent/pd/rpb180.pdf

Chapter 3
13. The Memory Management Glossary. http://www.memorymanagement.org/glossary/m.html
14. www.intel.com
15. G. C. Stierhoff and A. G. Davis. A History of the IBM Systems Journal. IEEE Annals of the History of Computing, Vol. 20, No. 1 (Jan. 1998), pages 29-35

Chapter 4
16. [http://www.pctechguide.com/21Architecture_DIB.htm]
17. [www.intel.com]
18. [http://ieeexplore.ieee.org/servlet/opac?punumber=4335 Ieee Standard Microcomputer System Bus]
19. [http://www.digitalprosound.com/Htm/TechStuff/June/SCSIvIDE-P2_1.htm]
20. [http://www.seagate.com/support/kb/disc/ultra2.html]
21. [http://en.wikipedia.org/wiki/Bus_topology]
22. [http://www.pctechguide.com/21Architecture_DIB.htm]

Chapter 5
23. [Stallings, Computer Organization and Architecture, Sixth Edition. by William Stallings.Prentice Hall]
24. [Tannenbaum a., Structured Computer Organisation, Prentice Hall, 2006]

Chapter 6

25. http://en.wikipedia.org/wiki/IA-32
26. MANOJ FRANKLIN, THE MULTISCALAR ARCHITECTURE, A thesis submitted in partial fulfillment of the requirements for the degree of DOCTOR OF PHILOSOPHY (Computer Sciences), UNIVERSITY OF WISCONSIN— MADISON, 1993
27. Georg Hager23 and Gerhard Wellein23, Architecture and Performance Characteristics of Modern High Performance Computers,   Springer Berlin / Heidelberg
28. https://stat.ethz.ch/pipermail/r-devel/2004-May/029658.html

Chapter 7

29. http://en.wikipedia.org/wiki/Flynn%27s_taxonomy
30. http://en.wikipedia.org/wiki/Vector_processor
31. http://carbon.cudenver.edu/~galaghba/simd.html
32. http://searchnetworking.techtarget.com/dictionary/definition/what-is-cross-bar-switch.html
33. http://www.cm.cf.ac.uk/Parallel/Year2/section5.html
34. Kaye RD, LSBU Lecture notes, Advanced computer architectures 2008
35. Top supercomputers, http://www.top500.org/
36. Parallel computing tutorial, https://computing.llnl.gov/tutorials/parallel_comp/#Models
37. Jaspal Subhlok, James M. Stichnoth, David R. O'hallaron, Thomas Gross, Exploiting Task and Data Parallelism on a Multicomputer (1993), ACM SIGPLAN Symposium on Principles and Practice of Parallel Programming, http://www.cs.uh.edu/~jaspal/papers/ppopp93.ps
38. Blaise Barney, Lawrence Livermore, Introduction to Parallel Computing, National Laboratory, https://computing.llnl.gov/tutorials/parallel_comp

Bibliography on the subject of parallel computing

39. Advances in Languages and Compilers for Parallel Processing. Edited by Alexandru Nicolau...[et al.]. Published by London: Pitman; Cambridge, Mass.: MIT Press, 1991.
40. Advances in Optimization and Parallel Computing: Honorary Volume on the Occasion of J.B. Rosen's 70th Birthday. Edited by Panos M. Pardalos. Published by Amsterdam; New York: North-Holland, 1992.
41. Advances in Parallel Computing. Published by Greenwich, Conn. : JAI Press, c1990,1992.
42. Advanced Topics in Dataflow Computing and Multithreading. Edited by Guang R. Gao, Lubomir Bic, Jean-Luc Gaudiot. Published by Los Alamitos, CA: IEEE Computer Society Press, c1995.
43. Associative Computing: A Programming Paradigm for Massively Parallel Computers. Written by Jerry L. Potter. Published by New York: Plenum Press, c 1992.
44. Multiprocessor Performance. Written by Erol Gelenbe. Published by Chichester; New York: Wiley, c1989.
45. Parallel Computation and Computers for Artificial Intelligence. Edited by Janusz S. Kowalik. Published by Boston: Kluwer Academic Publishers, c1988.
46. Parallel Computing: An Introduction. Written by Edward Lafferty....[et al.]. Published by Park Ridge, N.J. :Noyes Data Corp., c1993.
47. Parallel Supercomputing: Methods, Algorithms, and Applications. Edited by Graham F. Carey. Published by Chichester, West Sussex, England; New York: Wiley, c1989.
48. Past, Present, Parallel: A survey of Available Parallel Computer Systems. Edited by Arthur Trew and Greg Wilson. Published by London; New York : Springer-Verlag, c1991.

Appendix 1 Digital Electronic circuits

Introduction

All computer hardware is based on digital electronics. The digital here refers to signals that are not analogue. With analogue signals the amplitude varies with time. Digital signals use a number to represent amplitude.

In very simple terms an analogue signal is sampled digitally at a regular rate determined by the selected sampling period T. After a certain time t has passed we will have n samples of the signal. These values can be stored as numbers and processed accordingly. The electronic devices that are used to convert analogue signals to digital signals are called Analogue-to-Digital converters (ADCs). Conversely Digital to Analogue converters (DACs) are used to convert digital signals back to analogue.

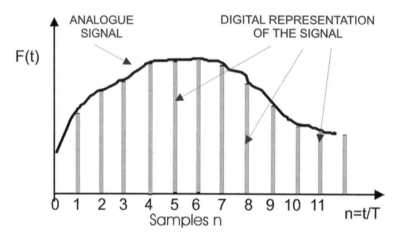

Figure A1.1 Digital representation of Analogue signals

In order to process digital signals it is necessary to select a suitable number system for their representation. The binary number system is very useful for digital signal representation because there are only two values in the number system, namely 0 and 1.

In a binary system, the number of bits that are needed to represent a value depends on how large this value is and also the required resolution. This is to say how accurately do we want the signal to be represented. For example, assume that the maximum amplitude of the analogue signal shown in figure A1.1 is 5V and we are using 8 bits to represent this signal in digital form (i.e. 8-bit resolution).

The smallest analogue value that we can represent in digital form is given by the following equation,

$$8-bit \Rightarrow \frac{5}{2^8} = \frac{5}{256} = 0.0195 \ Volts \ per \ bit \qquad (3.1)$$

On the other hand if 16-bit resolution were used the signal could be represented with the accuracy of,

$$16-bit \Rightarrow \frac{5}{2^{16}} = \frac{5}{65536} = 0.0000762 = 76.2 \times 10^{-6} \ Volts \ per \ bit$$

Evidently 16-bit is much more accurate than 8-bit but the question is whether this accuracy is required.

For example, assume that you need to represent the speed of your car using a digital tachometer. The maximum reading that you could possibly have is 300kph. Would you select 8-bit or 16-bit resolution to represent this reading.

Calculations: 8-bit resolution

$$Kph - per - bit = \frac{300}{2^8} = \frac{300}{256} = 1.172 \ kph \ per \ bit.$$

This means we can be accurate to roughly one kilometre per hour.

Calculations: 16-bit resolution

$$Kph - per - bit = \frac{300}{2^{16}} = \frac{300}{65536} = 0.0457 \ kph \ per \ bit.$$

This means that we can be accurate to within roughly 46 meters per hour.

The choice is yours, but if you consider that most digital speedometers do not display floating-point numbers, then 8-bit resolution might be more appropriate.

Therefore the number of bits that are used to represent the signal governs the resolution, or otherwise the accuracy of digital representation. To provide an idea how this works binary representation of the decimal equivalents are shown in the table below.

Table A1 Binary number representation

Decimal Number	Binary equivalent	Number of Bits used
3	11	2
255	11111111	8
254	11111110	8
65535	1111111111111111	16
4294967295	11111111111111111111111111111111	32

Here it is seen that two bits can be used to represent decimal numbers 0-5 inclusively. And also 32 bits can represent $2^{32}= 4,294,967,296$ numbers (in computer speak this is 4 Gig)

Because two is the base of the binary system, powers of two are important to computer science. Specifically, two to the power of n (i.e. 2^n)is the number of ways the bits in a binary integer of length n can be arranged. From table A1 it is seen that 2 bits can represent numbers from 0 to 3. That is $2^2=4$ individual combinations of bits. Thus it is seen that the numbers that are one less than a power of two denote the maximum values of integers in binary computers (one less because 0, and not 1, is the minimum value). Consequently, numbers of this form occur frequently in computer programs. For example a computer game running an 8-bit system, might limit the score the player can have a range 0-255. That is score has a maximum value of $2^8-1 = 255$.

The binary representation also allows us to use Boolean logic to process data. This enables digital circuits to compute that is to say to calculate values based on the signals received and the Boolean algebra operations that are performed. To make this possible digital logic codes its symbols in various ways: as voltages on wires (i.e. $0V -$

Low and *5V* – High used in TTL) in high-speed circuits and capacitive storage devices, as orientations of a magnetic domain in ferromagnetic storage devices (i.e. Floppy disks and magnetic tapes), as holes burned into a disk (i.e. CD-ROM) etc.

The digital electronic devices that are used to process these digital signals (codes) are numerous. The simplest of these are logic gates and the most complex are the central processing unit (CPU).

Logic gates

Boolean algebra is customarily based on logical counterparts to those operations, namely conjunction *x(AND)y,* disjunction *x(OR)y,* and complement or negation *x (NOT).* Another useful gate is the Exclusive OR, *x (XOR)y* gate, which is used in some special cases.

The codes that are used in these operations are fed into corresponding Logic Gates. Thus, we have different types of gates to complement the algebra. The most common gates are the **AND**, **OR** and **NOT** gates. **NAND** and **NOR** gates are the negated versions of the originals. The truth table is used to provide a relationship between the inputs and outputs for a given gate.

AND Gate	OR Gate	XOR Gate
Electronic Symbol		
x^*y	$x+y$	$x\oplus y$
Set Representation		
x^*y	$x+y$	$x\oplus y$
Truth Table		

x	y	$xANDy$
0	0	0
0	1	0
1	0	0
1	1	1

x	y	$xORy$
0	0	0
0	1	1
1	0	1
1	1	1

x	y	$xXORy$
0	0	0
0	1	1
1	0	1
1	1	0

The above diagram shows only two inputs, which in real terms would mean two bits. Larger number of bits can be considered. To make binary number representation easier to talk about a selected group of bits has a name. For example,

bit A single binary digit that can have either value 0 or 1.
byte 8 bits.
nibble 4 bits.
word 16 bits
double word 32 bits

In the above, the definition of "word" is not fixed because it has usually referred to the number of bits used in a register. These days, typical registers store 32 bits. However, already 64 bit architectures are being built (and have been for a few years).

This is the explanation from Wikipedia [Wiki]

Modern computers usually have a word size of 16, 32, or 64 bits. Sometimes the size of a word is defined to be a particular value for compatibility with earlier computers. The most common microprocessors used in personal computers (for instance, the Intel Pentiums and AMD Athlons) are an example of this. Their IA-32 architecture is an extension of the original Intel 8086 design, which had a word size of 16 bits. The IA-32 processors still support 8086 (x86) programs, so the meaning of "word" in the IA-32 context was kept the same, and is still said to be 16 bits, despite the fact that they may in actuality (and especially when the default operand size is 32-bit) operate more like a machine with a 32 bit word size. Similarly in the newer x86-64 architecture, a "word" is still 16 bits, although 64-bit ("quadruple word") operands may be more common.

Labelling Individual Bits

Bits are labelled from right to left in the increasing powers of two. The right-most bit is the Least Significant bit *(LSB)* and the left-most bit is the Most Significant Bit *(MSB)*. Thus as we move from right to left the number is doubled. This is quite convenient in binary arithmetic. You can multiply or divide a number by 2 simply by shifting it to the right or left. Table 3.2 shows an 8-bit (byte) representation.

	Bit 7	Bit 6	Bit 5	Bit 4	Bit 3	Bit 2	Bit 1	Bit 0
Power	2^7	2^6	2^5	2^4	2^3	2^2	2^1	2^0
Decimal Value	128	64	32	16	8	4	2	1

Thus for example, the byte *10101111* would have a decimal equivalent of 175.

	Bit 7	Bit 6	Bit 5	Bit 4	Bit 3	Bit 2	Bit 1	Bit 0
Power	2^7	2^6	2^5	2^4	2^3	2^2	2^1	2^0
Decimal Value	128	64	32	16	8	4	2	1
Binary value	1	0	1	0	1	1	1	1
	128	0	32	0	8	4	2	1

The sum of 128+32+8+4+2+1=175

Note that the maximum sum of an 8-bit number is 256, (i.e. 2^8=256) Namely,

	Bit 7	Bit 6	Bit 5	Bit 4	Bit 3	Bit 2	Bit 1	Bit 0
Power	2^7	2^6	2^5	2^4	2^3	2^2	2^1	2^0
Decimal Value	128	64	32	16	8	4	2	1
Binary value	1	1	1	1	1	1	1	1
	128	64	32	16	8	4	2	1

The sum of 128+64+32+16+8+4+2+1=175

It is clear that binary number representation is very useful in digital computing because it can be represented by two values only. Different number representation is sometimes used to help programmers so that they do not need to think in binary. Hexadecimal number representation works in base 16. This is convenient because 4 bits can represent 16 numbers (0 to 15 inclusive). Thus a half a byte (nibble) is needed to represent a hexadecimal number. Furthermore, because there are 16 of these in base 16, numbers *0-9* are used for values as in decimal, and characters *A-F* are used for the additional digits.

Therefore the hexadecimal numbers are represented as shown in table A.2. Here the binary numbers are show as nibbles. Remember that two nibbles make a byte and consequently two hexadecimal numbers make a byte too.

Table A.2

Hex	Dec	Bin
0	0	0000
1	1	0001
2	2	0010
3	3	0011
4	4	0100
5	5	0101
6	6	0110
7	7	0111
8	8	1000
9	9	1001
A	10	1010
B	11	1011
C	12	1100
D	13	1101
E	14	1110
F	15	1111

Bitstrings and Bit vectors
http://www.cs.umd.edu/class/spring2003/cmsc311/Notes/Data/bitBytes.html

While there are standard sizes for differing number of bits (bits, bytes, nibbles, etc.), sometimes you just need to refer to a more arbitrary set of bits. We'll refer to a "N" bits as a bitstring or a bit vector.

It may seem odd to refer to a number as a string, but it's not so unusual. When you write numbers, you typically increase the number of digits as needed. Thus, you write 10, instead of 0010. However, in hardware, you often have a fixed number of bits, such as 16 bits or 32 bits. Leading zeroes will always appear to pad it to the necessary number of total bits.

So, the name "bit string" might be just as good any because it may imply a length of a string.

Bitstrings are also called bit vectors. In this case, a vector typically means a "coordinate" with N arguments. For example, when you study graphs in 2 or 3 dimensions, coordinates are written like (2,3) or (2,3,1). So 0010 could be thought of as (0,0,1,0), i.e. a coordinate in four dimensions.

Of course, when people talk about bit vectors, they're generally not thinking about it as a coordinate. The main point is that, unlike sets, vectors have numbered positions (though typically, vectors are numbered left to right, starting at index 1).

The number of unique bitstring patterns available (lets call it k) is a function of the number of bits n, such that $k=2^n$. Table 3.3 shows the bitstring patterns for a 3-bit bitstring.

Bitstring			
Bit 2	Bit 1	Bit 0	*Decimal*
2^2	2^1	2^0	*value*
0	0	0	0
0	0	1	1
0	1	0	2
0	1	1	3
1	0	0	4
1	0	1	5
1	1	0	6
1	1	1	7

For 3 bits, you have $2^3=8$ possible bitstring patterns. That limits you to a maximum of 8 different values.

This works in reverse also, such that you may ask yourself the following question. How many bits do I need to represent N different items.

Suppose you have **N** different items. You wish to label them with **K** bit binary number. We know that if we have **K** bits, then there are 2^K different bitstring patterns. Thus, we want to solve:

$$2^k \geq N$$

To solve this, we take lg of both sides (this is log base two).
lg(2K) >= lg(N)
which simplifies to:

K >= lg(N)

which we can write as

K = ceil(lg(N))

The ceiling of X is the integer value Y such that Y - 1 < X <= Y. Thus, you round X up to the next highest integer, unless X is already an integer.

Why is this problem important? In a CPU, we will need to find some way to identify registers. Since computers manipulate 0's and 1's, we assign each register to a unique binary number.

Thus, if we have 32 registers, we assign each register a ceil(lg(32)) = 5 bit number. If the number of registers is not a power of 2, say, there are 12 registers, then we use ceil(lg(12)) = 4 bits.

In particular, we usually assign the registers an unsigned binary number starting at 0 and ending at N - 1.

For 12 registers, we assign 0000two (which is 0ten) up to 1011two (which is 11ten). The other four bitstring patterns (from 1100two to 1111two) are unused.

So if you're asked how many bits does it take to identify N different items, the answer is the ceiling of the lg (base two) of N.

This is one of those REALLY IMPORTANT FACTS (TM) that you should know.

Difference between Combinational and Sequential Logic

http://www.cs.umd.edu/class/spring2003/cmsc311/Notes/Seq/diff.html

Flip Flops

Introduction

Combinational logic circuits implement Boolean functions. Boolean functions are mappings of input bit strings to output bit strings. These circuits are functions of input only. This means that if you feed in an input to a circuit, say, 000, then look at its output, and discover it is, say, 10, then the output will always be 10 for that circuit, if 000 is the input. In other words 000 is mapped to 10.

If that value were not the same every single time, then the output must not completely depend on 000. Something else must be affecting the output. Combinational logic circuits always depend on input.

Another way to define something that is a function of input is to imagine that you are only allowed to use input variables $x_{k-1},...,x_0$, i.e. data inputs or $c_{m-1},...,c_0$, i.e., control inputs, to write the function. This function cannot depend on global variables or other variables.

Example: Snack vending machine

Snack vending machine have been in use for some time, and typically these machines would accept an input of coins corresponding to a value of the snack and when the inputs satisfy the required value a snack is dispensed. Let us then consider if this machine is functional (i.e., behaves like a mathematical function). In other words, we wish to ascertain its output is solely dependent on the input.

Assume that this machine only sells Mars bars, and that the price of a Mars bar is 40 pence. Furthermore, assume that it can only take 10p coins. Once 40p is deposited, a Mars bar is dispensed. You don't even have to press a button.

To buy a Mars bar you place the first coin in the machine, and out comes...nothing!, you put another 10p in, and out comes....nothing!, you decide to put in yet another 10p, and still nothing comes out, you put another 10p and out comes a Mars bar. So is this machine functional? To answer this question, think about how the machine behaved. You gave the same input, four times in a row, but it did not produce the same output, four times in a row. Three times it produced nothing and the fourth time it produced a Mars bar.

A mathematical function maps inputs to outputs. Thus, once you know what the input maps to, that should be it. In this case, the input (a 10p coin) mapped to nothing, nothing, nothing, and a Mars bar. So, clearly, this does not behave like a function.

Clearly, the machine is storing some information. In particular, it's records how much money you have entered so far. The output is determined not only by the input, but also by this stored information.

This stored information is an example of **state** which is basically the internal information concerning an object that can change as the object is used. To explain these consider, for example, that you have a linked list called **list**. You call **list.size()**. Does that method call always return the same value? The answer is no. The method call will return the current size of the linked list, which may change over time, as elements are added or removed from the list. Thus, the method is computing its value not only on the input (and there is none, since the **size()** method requires no arguments), but also based on the number of nodes in the object.

You can think of the data members as state. It is internal information recorded by the object. Any method does its computation based on the arguments passed in and based on the values of the data members.

Sequential Circuits

For this course, we represent states by a **k-bit** UB number. Given **k** bits, we can have up to 2^k different states.

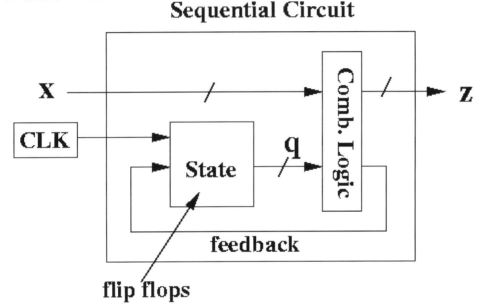

Sequential Circuit

Here are some of the key things to notice:

- Like combinational logic circuits, a sequential logic circuit has inputs (labelled with **x** with subscripts) and outputs (labelled with **z** with subscripts).
- Unlike combinational logic circuits, a sequential logic circuit uses a *clock*.
- Also, there is a box inside the circuit called **State**.
- This box contains flip-flops. Assume it has **k** flip-flops. The flip-flops basically store a k-bit number representing the current state.
- The output **z** is computed based on the inputs (**x** with subscripts) and the state coming out of the state box (**q** with subscripts).
- The state may be updated at each positive clock edge. When there's not a positive clock edge, the state remains unchanged.
- The information needed to update to the state (called the *next state*) comes from the current state (the current value of **q**) and the input, which is fed through combinational logic, and fed back into the state box, telling the state box how to update itself.

For example, suppose you are currently in state 00, and see an input of 1. This may produce an output of, say, 10, and then produce feedback that tells the state box to update to state 01 by the next clock edge.

Summary

A sequential circuit uses flip-flops. Unlike combinational logic, sequential circuits have state, which means basically, sequential circuits have memory.

The diagram shown earlier is one way to model sequential circuits. They can be modelled as finite state machines. We'll describe those in more detail in a future set of notes, so if you don't understand it, that's OK. It should be clearer in a future set of notes.

The main difference between sequential circuits and combinational circuits is that sequential circuits compute their output based on input and state, and that the state is updated based on a clock. Combinational logic circuits implement Boolean functions, so they are functions only of their inputs, and are not based on clocks.

APPENDIX 2 DESIGNING A CPU

This appendix contains a document that has been sourced from the following URL on 5/3/2008.
http://www.faqs.org/docs/Linux-HOWTO/s11
It is included here for reader's convenience and it is freely available form the above URL.
I have included the copyright notice and I have not modified the article in any way.

CPU DESIGN HOW-TO

Al Dev (Alavoor Vasudevan) alavoor[AT]yahoo.com

v12.5, 17 Feb 2002

CPU is the "brain" of computer and is a very vital component of computer system and is like a "cousin brother" of operating system (Linux or Unix). This document helps companies, businesses, universities and research institutes to design, build and manufacture CPUs. Also the information will be useful for university students of U.S.A and Canada who are studying computer science/engineering. The document has URL links, which helps students understand how a CPU is designed and manufactured. Perhaps in near future there will be a GNU/GPLed CPU running Linux, Unix, Microsoft Windows, Apple Mac and BeOS operating systems!!

---

1. Introduction

2. What is IP ?

- 2.1 Free CPU List
- 2.2 Commercial CPU List

3. CPU Museum and Silicon Zoo

- 3.1 CPU Museum
- 3.2 How Transistors work
- 3.3 How a Transistors handles information
- 3.4 Displaying binary information
- 3.5 What is a Semi-conductor?

4. CPU Design and Architecture

- 4.1 CPU Design
- 4.2 Online Textbooks on CPU Architecture
- 4.3 University Lecture notes on CPU Architecture
- 4.4 CPU Architecture
- 4.5 Usenet Newsgroups for CPU design

5. Fabrication, Manufacturing CPUs

6. Super Computer Architecture

7. Linux Super Computers

8. Neural Network Processors

9. Related URLs

10. Other Formats of this Document

11. Copyright

---

1. Introduction

(The latest version of this document is at http://www.milkywaygalaxy.freeservers.com. You may want to check there for changes).

This document provides you comprehensive list of URLs for CPU Design and fabrication. Using this information students, companies, universities or businesses can make new CPUs, which can run Linux/Unix operating systems.

In olden days, chip vendors were also the IP developers and the EDA tools developers. Nowadays, we have specialized fab companies (TSMC http://www.tsmc.com), IP companies (ARM http://www.arm.com, MIPS http://www.mips.com, Gray Research LLC http://cnets.sourceforge.net/grllc.html), and tools companies (Mentor http://www.mentor.com, Cadence http://www.cadence.com, etc.), and combinations of these (Intel). You can buy IP bundled with hardware (Intel), bundled with your tools (EDA companies), or separately (IP providers).

Enter the FPGA vendors (Xilinx http://www.xilinx.com, Altera http://www.altera.com). They have an opportunity to seize upon a unique business model.

VA Linux systems http://www.valinux.com builds the entire system and perhaps in future will design and build CPUs for Linux.

Visit the following CPU design sites:

- FPGA CPU Links http://www.fpgacpu.org/links.html
- FPGA Main site http://www.fpgacpu.org
- OpenRISC 1000 Free Open-source 32-bit RISC processor IP core competing with proprietary ARM and MIPS is at http://www.opencores.org
- Open IP org http://www.openip.org
- Free IP org - ASIC and FPGA cores for masses http://www.free-ip.com

---

2. What is IP ?

What is IP ? IP is short for **Intellectual Property**. More specifically, it is a block of logic that can be used in making ASIC's and FPGA's. Examples of "IP Cores" are, UART's, CPU's, Ethernet Controllers, PCI Interfaces, etc. In the past, quality cores of this nature could cost anywhere from US$5,000 to more than US$350,000. This is way too high for the average company or individual to even contemplate using -- Hence, the Free-IP project.

Initially the Free-IP project will focus on the more complex cores, like CPU's and Ethernet controllers. Less complex cores might follow.

The Free-IP project is an effort to make quality IP available to anyone.

Visit the following sites for IP cores -

- Open IP org http://www.openip.org
- Free IP org - ASIC and FPGA cores for masses http://www.free-ip.com
- FPGA Main site http://www.fpgacpu.org

2.1 Free CPU List

Here is the list of Free CPUs available or currently under development -

- F-CPU 64-bit Freedom CPU http://www.f-cpu.org mirror site at http://www.f-cpu.de
- SPARC Organisation http://www.sparc.org
- SPARC International http://www.sparc.com
- European Space Agency - SPARC architecture LEON CPU http://www.estec.esa.nl/wsmwww/leon
- European Space Agency - ERC32 SPARC V7 CPU http://www.estec.esa.nl/wsmwww/erc32
- Atmel ERC32 SPARC part # TSC695E http://www.atmel-wm.com/products click on Aerospace=>Space=>Processors

- Sayuri at http://www.morphyplanning.co.jp/Products/FreeCPU/freecpu-e.html and manufactured by Morphy Planning Ltd at http://www.morphyone.org and feature list at http://ds.dial.pipex.com/town/plaza/aj93/waggy/hp/features/morphyone.htm and in Japanese language at http://www.morphyplanning.or.jp
- OpenRISC 1000 Free 32-bit processor IP core competing with proprietary ARM and MIPS is at http://www.opencores.org/cores/or1k
- OpenRISC 2000 is at http://www.opencores.org
- STM 32-bit, 2-way superscalar RISC CPU http://www.asahi-net.or.jp/~uf8e-itu
- Green Mountain - GM HC11 CPU Core is at http://www.gmvhdl.com/hc11core.html
- Open-source CPU site - Google Search "Computers>Hardware>Open Source" http://directory.google.com/Top/Computers/Hardware/Open_Source
- Free microprocessor and DSP IP cores written in Verilog or VHDL http://www.cmosexod.com
- Free hardware cores to speed development http://www.scrap.de/html/opencore.htm
- Linux open hardware and free EDA systems http://opencollector.org

2.2 Commercial CPU List

- Russian E2K 64-bit CPU (Very fast CPU !!!) website : http://www.elbrus.ru/roadmap/e2k.html. **ELBRUS** is now partnered (alliance) with Sun Microsystems of USA.
- Korean CPU from Samsung 64-bit CPU original from DEC Alpha http://www.samsungsemi.com Alpha-64bit CPU is at http://www.alpha-processor.com Now there is collaboration between Samsumg, Compaq of USA on Alpha CPU
- Intel IA 64 http://developer.intel.com/design/ia-64
- Transmeta crusoe CPU and in near future Transmeta's 64-bit CPU http://www.transmeta.com
- Sun Ultra-sparc 64-bit CPU http://www.sun.com or http://www.sunmicrosystems.com
- HAL-Fujitsu (California) Super-Sparc 64-bit processor http://www.hal.com also compatible to Sun's sparc architecture.
- SPARC Organisation http://www.sparc.org
- SPARC International http://www.sparc.com
- MIPS RISC CPUs http://www.mips.com
- Silicon Graphics MIPS Architecture CPUs http://www.sgi.com/processors
- IDT MIPS Architecture CPUs http://www.idt.com
- IBM Power PC (motorola) http://www.motorola.com/SPS/PowerPC/index.html
- Motorola embedded processors. SPS processor based on PowerPC, M-CORE, ColdFire, M68k, or M68HC cores http://www.mot-sps.com
- Hitachi SuperH 64-bit RISC processor SH7750 http://www.hitachi.com sold at $40 per CPU in quantities of 10,000. Hitachi SH4,3,2,1 CPUs http://semiconductor.hitachi.com/superh
- Fujitsu 64-bit processor http://www.fujitsu.com
- Seimens Pyramid CPU from Pyramid Technologies
- Intel X86 series 32-bit CPUs Pentiums, Celeron etc..
- AMDs X86 series 32-bit CPUs K-6, Athlon etc..
- National's Cyrix X86 series 32-bit CPUs Cyrix etc..
- ARC CPUs : http://www.arccores.com

- QED RISC 64-bit and MIPS cpus : http://www.qedinc.com/about.htm
- Origin 2000 CPU - http://techpubs.sgi.com/library/manuals/3000/007-3511-001/html/O2000Tuning.1.html
- NVAX CPUs http://www.research.compaq.com/wrl/DECarchives/DTJ/DTJ700 and at mirror-site
- Univ. of Mich High-perf. GaAs Microprocessor Project http://www.eecs.umich.edu/UMichMP
- Hyperstone E1-32 RISC/DSP processor http://bwrc.eecs.berkeley.edu/CIC/tech/hyperstone
- PSC1000 32-bit RISC processor http://www.ptsc.com/psc1000/index.html
- IDT R/RV4640 and R/RV4650 64-bit CPU w/DSP Capability http://www.idt.com/products/pages/Processors-PL100_Sub205_Dev128.html
- ARM CPU http://www.arm.com/Documentation
- Cogent CPUs http://www.cogcomp.com
- CPU Info center - List of CPUs sparc, arm etc.. http://bwrc.eecs.berkeley.edu/CIC/tech
- Main CPU site is : Google Search engine CPU site "Computers>Hardware>Components>Microprocessors" http://directory.google.com/Top/Computers/Hardware/Components/Microprocessors

Other important CPU sites are at -

- World-wide 24-hour news on CPUs http://www.newsnow.co.uk/cgi/NewsNow/NewsLink.htm?Theme=Processors
- The computer architecture site is at http://www.cs.wisc.edu/~arch/www
- ARM CPU http://www.arm.com/Documentation
- Great CPUs http://www.cs.uregina.ca/~bayko/cpu.html
- Microdesign resources http://www.mdronline.com

---

3. CPU Museum and Silicon Zoo

This chapter gives very basics of CPU technology. If you have good technical background then you can skip this entire chapter.

3.1 CPU Museum

CPU Museum is at

- Intel CPU Museum http://www.intel.com/intel/intelis/museum
- Intel - History of Microprocessors http://www.intel.com/intel/museum/25anniv
- Virtual Museum of Computing http://www.museums.reading.ac.uk/vmoc
- Silicon Zoo http://micro.magnet.fsu.edu/creatures/index.html
- Intel - How the Microprocessors work http://www.intel.com/education/mpuworks
- Simple course in Microprocessors http://www.hkrmicro.com/course/micro.html

3.2 How Transistors work

Microprocessors are essential to many of the products we use every day such as TVs, cars, radios, home appliances and of course, computers. Transistors are the main components of microprocessors. At their most basic level, transistors may seem simple. But their development actually required many years of painstaking research. Before transistors, computers relied on slow, inefficient vacuum tubes and mechanical switches to process information. In 1958, engineers (one of them Intel founder Robert Noyce) managed to put two transistors onto a silicon crystal and create the first integrated circuit that led to the microprocessor.

Transistors are miniature electronic switches. They are the building blocks of the microprocessor, which is the brain of the computer. Similar to a basic light switch, transistors have two operating positions, on and off. This on/off, or binary functionality of transistors enables the processing of information in a computer.

How a simple electronic switch works:

The only information computers understand is electrical signals that are switched on and off. To comprehend transistors, it is necessary to have an understanding of how a switched electronic circuit works. Switched electronic circuits consist of several parts. One is the circuit pathway where the electrical current flows - typically through a wire. Another is the switch, a device that starts and stops the flow of electrical current by either completing or breaking the circuit's pathway. Transistors have no moving parts and are turned on and off by electrical signals. The on/off switching of transistors facilitates the work performed by microprocessors.

3.3 How a Transistors handles information

Something that has only two states, like a transistor, can be referred to as binary. A 1 represents the transistor's on state and a 0 represents the off state. Specific sequences and patterns of 1's and 0's generated by multiple transistors can represent letters, numbers, colours and graphics. This is known as binary notation

3.4 Displaying binary information

Spell your name in Binary:

Each character of the alphabet has a binary equivalent. Below is the name JOHN and its equivalent in binary.

J 0100 1010
O 0100 1111
H 0100 1000
N 0100 1110

More complex information can be created such as graphics, audio and video using the binary, or on/off action of transistors.

Scroll down to the Binary Chart below to see the complete alphabet in binary.

Binary Chart for Alphabets			
Character	Binary	Character	Binary
A	0100 0001	N	0100 1110
B	0100 0010	O	0100 1111
C	0100 0011	P	0101 0000
D	0100 0100	Q	0101 0001
E	0100 0101	R	0101 0010
F	0100 0110	S	0101 0011
G	0100 0111	T	0101 0100
H	0100 1000	U	0101 0101
I	0100 1001	V	0101 0110
J	0100 1010	W	0101 0111
K	0100 1011	X	0101 1000
L	0100 1100	Y	0101 1001
M	0100 1101	Z	0101 1010

3.5 What is a Semi-conductor?

Conductors and insulators :

Many materials, such as most metals, allow electrical current to flow through them. These are known as conductors. Materials that do not allow electrical current to flow through them are called insulators. Pure silicon, the base material of most transistors, is considered a semiconductor because its conductivity can be modulated by the introduction of impurities.

Anatomy of Transistor

Semiconductors and flow of electricity

Adding certain types of impurities to the silicon in a transistor changes its crystalline structure and enhances its ability to conduct electricity. Silicon containing boron impurities is called p-type silicon - p for positive or lacking electrons. Silicon containing phosphorus impurities is called n-type silicon - n for negative or having a majority of free electrons

A Working Transistor

A Working transistor - The On/Off state of Transistor

Transistors consist of three terminals; the source, the gate and the drain.

In the n-type transistor, both the source and the drain are negatively charged and sit on a positively charged well of p-silicon.

When positive voltage is applied to the gate, electrons in the p-silicon are attracted to the area under the gate forming an electron channel between the source and the drain.

When positive voltage is applied to the drain, the electrons are pulled from the source to the drain. In this state the transistor is on.

If the voltage at the gate is removed, electrons aren't attracted to the area between the source and drain. The pathway is broken and the transistor is turned off.

Impact of Transistors

The Impact of Transistors - How microprocessors affect our lives.

The binary function of transistors gives micro- processors the ability to perform many tasks; from simple word processing to video editing. Micro- processors have evolved to a point where transistors can execute hundreds of millions of instructions per second on a single chip. Automobiles, medical devices, televisions, computers and even the Space Shuttle use microprocessors. They all rely on the flow of binary information made possible by the transistor.

---

4. CPU Design and Architecture

4.1 CPU Design

Visit the following links for information on CPU Design.

- Hamburg University VHDL archive http://tech-www.informatik.uni-hamburg.de/vhdl
- Kachina Design tools http://SAL.KachinaTech.COM/Z/1/index.shtml
- List of FPGA-based Computing Machines http://www.io.com/~guccione/HW_list.html
- SPARC Organisation http://www.sparc.org
- SPARC International http://www.sparc.com
- Design your own processor http://www.spacetimepro.com
- Teaching Computer Design with FPGAs http://www.fpgacpu.org
- Technical Committee on Computer Architecture http://www.computer.org/tab/tcca
- Frequently Asked Questions FAQ on VHDL http://www.vhdl.org/vi/comp.lang.vhdl or it is at http://www.vhdl.org/comp.lang.vhdl
- Comp arch FAQ http://www.esacademy.com/automation/faq.htm
- Comp arch FAQ ftp://rtfm.mit.edu/pub/usenet-by-hierarchy/comp/arch
- VME Bus FAQ http://www.hitex.com/automation/FAQ/vmefaq

- Homepage of SPEC http://performance.netlib.org/performance/html/spec.html
- Linux benchmarks http://www.silkroad.com/linux-bm.html

4.2 Online Textbooks on CPU Architecture

- Online HTML book http://odin.ee.uwa.edu.au/~morris/CA406/CA_ToC.html
- Univ of Texas Comp arch :
  http://www.cs.panam.edu/~meng/Course/CS4335/Notes/master/master.html
- Number systems and Logic circuits :
  http://www.tpub.com/neets/book13/index.htm
- Digital Logic: http://www.play-hookey.com/digital
- Flip-Flops:
  http://www.ece.utexas.edu/~cjackson/FlipFlops/web_pages/Publish/FlipFlops.
  html
- Instruction Execution cycle: http://cq-pan.cqu.edu.au/students/timp1/exec.html
- Truth Table constructor: http://pirate.shu.edu/~borowsbr/Truth/Truth.html
- Overview of Shared Memory: http://www.sics.se/cna/mp_overview.html
- Simultaneous Multi-threading in processors :
  http://www.cs.washington.edu/research/smt
- Study Web : http://www.studyweb.com/links/277.html
- Univ notes: http://www.ece.msstate.edu/~linder/Courses/EE4713/notes
- Advice: An Adaptable and Extensible Distributed Virtual Memory Architecture
  http://www.gsyc.inf.uc3m.es/~nemo/export/adv-pdcs96/adv-pdcs96.html
- Univ of Utah Avalanche Scalable Parallel Processor Project
  http://www.cs.utah.edu/avalanche/avalanche-publications.html
- Distributed computing :
  http://www.geocities.com/SiliconValley/Vista/4015/pdcindex.html
- Pisma Memory architecture: http://aiolos.cti.gr/en/pisma/pisma.html
- Shared Mem Arch: http://www.ncsa.uiuc.edu/General/Exemplar/ARPA
- Textbooks on Comp Arch:
  http://www.rdrop.com/~cary/html/computer_architecture.html#book and VLSI
  design http://www.rdrop.com/~cary/html/vlsi.html
- Comp Arch Conference and Journals
  http://www.handshake.de/user/kroening/conferences.html
- WWW Comp arch page http://www.cs.wisc.edu/~arch/www

4.3 University Lecture notes on CPU Architecture

- Advanced Computer Architecture
  http://www.cs.utexas.edu/users/dahlin/Classes/GradArch
- Computer architecture - Course level 415
  http://www.diku.dk/teaching/2000f/f00.415
- MIT: http://www.csg.lcs.mit.edu/6.823
- UBC CPU slides :
  http://www.cs.ubc.ca/spider/neufeld/courses/cs218/chapter8/index.htm
- Purdue Univ slides:
  http://www.ece.purdue.edu/~gba/ee565/Sessions/S03HTML/index.htm
- Rutgers Univ - Principles of Comp Arch :
  http://www.cs.rutgers.edu/~murdocca/POCA/Chapter02.html
- Brown Univ - http://www.engin.brown.edu/faculty/daniels/DDZO/cmparc.html
- Univ of Sydney - Intro Digital Systems :
  http://www.eelab.usyd.edu.au/digital_tutorial/part3

- Bournemouth Univ, UK Principles of Computer Systems :
  http://ncca.bournemouth.ac.uk/CourseInfo/BAVisAn/Year1/CompSys
- Parallel Virtual machine: http://www.netlib.org/pvm3/book/node1.html
- univ center: http://www.eecs.lehigh.edu/~mschulte/ece401-99
- univ course: http://www.cs.utexas.edu/users/fussell/cs352
- Examples of working VLSI circuits(in Greek)
  http://students.ceid.upatras.gr/~gef/projects/vlsi

4.4 CPU Architecture

Visit the following links for information on CPU architecture

- Comp architecture: http://www.rdrop.com/~cary/html/computer_architecture.html
  and VLSI design http://www.rdrop.com/~cary/html/vlsi.html
- Beyond RISC - The Post-RISC Architecture
  http://www.cps.msu.edu/~crs/cps920
- Beyond RISC - PostRISC : http://www.ceng.metu.edu.tr/~e106170/postrisc.html
- List of CPUS http://einstein.et.tudelft.nl/~offerman/cl.contents2.html
- PowerPC Arch
  http://www.mactech.com/articles/mactech/Vol.10/10.08/PowerPcArchitecture
- CPU Info center - List of CPUs sparc, arm etc..
  http://bwrc.eecs.berkeley.edu/CIC/tech
- cpu arch intel IA 64 http://developer.intel.com/design/ia-64
- Intel 386 CPU architecture http://www.delorie.com/djgpp/doc/ug/asm/about-
  386.html
- Freedom CPU architecture http://f-cpu.tux.org/original/Freedom.php3
- Z80 CPU architecture
  http://www.geocities.com/SiliconValley/Peaks/3938/z80arki.htm
- CRIMSEN OS and teaching-aid CPU
  http://www.dcs.gla.ac.uk/~ian/project3/node1.html
- Assembly Language concepts
  http://www.cs.uaf.edu/~cs301/notes/Chapter1/node1.html
- Alpha CPU architecture http://www.linux3d.net/cpu/CPU/alpha/index.shtml
- http://hugsvr.kaist.ac.kr/~exit/cpu.html
- Tron CPU architecture http://tronweb.super-nova.co.jp/tronvlsicpu.html

4.5 Usenet Newsgroups for CPU design

- Newsgroup computer architecture news:comp.arch
- Newsgroup FPGA news:comp.arch.fpga
- Newsgroup Arithmetic news:comp.arch.arithmetic
- Newsgroup Bus news:comp.arch.bus
- Newsgroup VME Bus news:comp.arch.vmebus
- Newsgroup embedded news:comp.arch.embedded
- Newsgroup embedded piclist news:comp.arch.embedded.piclist
- Newsgroup storage news:comp.arch.storage
- Newsgroup VHDL news:comp.lang.vhdl
- Newsgroup Computer Benchmarks news:comp.benchmarks

5. Fabrication, Manufacturing CPUs

After doing the design and testing of CPU, your company may want to mass-produce the CPUs. There are many "semi-conductor foundries" in the world who will do that for you for a nominal competitive cost. There are companies in USA, Germany, UK, Japan, Taiwan, Korea and China.

TMSC (Taiwan) is the **"largest independent foundry"** in the world. You may want to shop around and you will get the best rate for a very high volume production (greater than 100,000 CPU units).

5.1 Foundry Business is in Billions of dollars!!

Foundry companies invested very heavily in the infrastructure and building plants runs in several millions of dollars! Silicon foundry business will grow from $7 billion to $36 billion by 2004 (414% increase!!). More integrated device manufacturers (IDMs) opt to outsource chip production verses adding wafer-processing capacity.

Independent foundries currently produce about 12% of the semiconductors in the world, and by 2004, that share will more than double to 26%.

The "Big Three" pure-play foundries in the whole world are:

1. Taiwan Semiconductor Manufacturing Co. (TSMC)
2. United Microelectronics Corp. (UMC)
3. Chartered Semiconductor Manufacturing Ltd. Pte.

These three companies collectively account for 69% of today's silicon foundry volume, but their share is expected to grow to 88% by 2004. These percentages exclude those companies, which are not "pure-play foundries" like Intel, IBM and others who have in-house foundries for self-production of wafers.

5.2 Fabrication of CPU

There are hundreds of foundries in the world (too numerous to list). Some of them are -

- Fabless Semiconductor Association http://www.fsa.org
- TSMC (Taiwan Semi-conductor Manufacturing Co) http://www.tsmc.com, about co http://www.tsmc.com/about/index.html
- Chartered Semiconductor Manufacturing, Singapore http://www.csminc.com
- United Microelectronics Corp. (UMC) http://www.umc.com/index.html
- Advanced BGA Packing http://www.abpac.com
- Amcor, Arizona http://www.amkor.com
- Elume, USA http://www.elume.com
- X-Fab, Gesellschaft zur Fertigung von Wafern mbH, Erfurt, Germany http://www.xfab.com
- IBM corporation, (Semi-conductor foundry div) http://www.ibm.com
- National Semi-conductor Co, Santa Clara, USA http://www.natioanl.com
- Tower Semiconductor, San Jose, USA http://www.towersemi.com
- Intel corporation (Semi-conductor foundries), USA http://www.intel.com
- Hitachi Semi-conductor Co, Japan http://www.hitachi.com

- FUJITSU limited, Japan has Wafer-foundry-services
- Mitsubhishi Semi-conductor Co, Japan
- Hyandai Semi-conductor, Korea http://www.hea.com
- Samsumg Semi-conductor, Korea
- Atmel, France http://www.atmel-wm.com

If you know any major foundries, let me know I will add to list.

List of CHIP foundry companies

- Chip directory http://www.xs4all.nl/~ganswijk/chipdir/make/foundry.htm
- Chip makers http://www.xs4all.nl/~ganswijk/chipdir/make/index.htm
- IC manufacturers http://www.xs4all.nl/~ganswijk/chipdir/c/a.htm

---

6. Super Computer Architecture

For building Super computers, the trend that seems to emerge is that most new systems look as minor variations on the same theme: clusters of RISC-based Symmetric Multi-Processing (SMP) nodes which in turn are connected by a fast network. Consider this as a natural architectural evolution. The availability of relatively low-cost (RISC) processors and network products to connect these processors together with standardised communication software has stimulated the building of home-brew clusters computers as an alternative to complete systems offered by vendors.

Visit the following sites for Super Computers -

- Top 500 super computers http://www.top500.org/ORSC/2000
- National Computing Facilities Foundation http://www.nwo.nl/ncf/indexeng.htm
- Linux Super Computer Beowulf cluster http://www.tldp.org/HOWTO/Beowulf-HOWTO.html
- Extreme machines - beowulf cluster http://www.xtreme-machines.com
- System architecture description of the Hitachi SR2201 http://www.hitachi.co.jp/Prod/comp/hpc/eng/sr1.html
- Personal Parallel Supercomputers http://www.checs.net/checs_98/papers/super

6.1 Main Architectural Classes

Before going on to the descriptions of the machines themselves, it is important to consider some mechanisms that are or have been used to increase the performance. The hardware structure or architecture determines to a large extent what the possibilities and impossibilities are in speeding up a computer system beyond the performance of a single CPU. Another important factor that is considered in combination with the hardware is the capability of compilers to generate efficient code to be executed on the given hardware platform. In many cases it is hard to distinguish between hardware and software influences and one has to be careful in the interpretation of results when ascribing certain effects to hardware or software peculiarities or both. In this chapter we will give most emphasis to the hardware architecture. For a description of machines that can be considered to be classified as "high-performance".

Since many years the taxonomy of Flynn has proven to be useful for the classification of high-performance computers. This classification is based on the way of manipulating of instruction and data streams and comprises four main architectural classes. We will first briefly sketch these classes and afterwards fill in some details when each of the classes is described.

6.2 SISD machines

These are the conventional systems that contain one CPU and hence can accommodate one instruction stream that is executed serially. Nowadays many large mainframes may have more than one CPU but each of these execute instruction streams that are unrelated. Therefore, such systems still should be regarded as (a couple of) SISD machines acting on different data spaces. Examples of SISD machines are for instance most workstations like those of DEC, Hewlett-Packard, and Sun Microsystems. The definition of SISD machines is given here for completeness' sake. We will not discuss this type of machines in this report.

6.3 SIMD machines

Such systems often have a large number of processing units, ranging from 1,024 to 16,384 that all may execute the same instruction on different data in lock step. So, a single instruction manipulates many data items in parallel. Examples of SIMD machines in this class are the CPP DAP Gamma II and the Alenia Quadrics.

Another subclass of the SIMD systems are the vector processors. Vector processors act on arrays of similar data rather than on single data items using specially structured CPUs. When data can be manipulated by these vector units, results can be delivered with a rate of one, two and --- in special cases --- of three per clock cycle (a clock cycle being defined as the basic internal unit of time for the system). So, vector processors execute on their data in an almost parallel way but only when executing in vector mode. In this case they are several times faster than when executing in conventional scalar mode. For practical purposes vector processors are therefore mostly regarded as SIMD machines. Examples of such systems is for instance the Hitachi S3600.

6.4 MISD machines

Theoretically in these types of machines multiple instructions should act on a single stream of data. As yet no practical machine in this class has been constructed nor are such systems easily to conceive. We will disregard them in the following discussions.

6.5 MIMD machines

These machines execute several instruction streams in parallel on different data. The difference with the multi-processor SISD machines mentioned above lies in the fact that the instructions and data are related because they represent different parts of the same task to be executed. So, MIMD systems may run many sub-tasks in parallel in order to shorten the time-to-solution for the main task to be executed. There are a large variety of MIMD systems and especially in this class the Flynn taxonomy proves to be not fully adequate for the classification of systems. Systems that behave very differently like a four-processor NEC SX-5 and a thousand processor SGI/Cray T3E fall both in this class. In the following we will make another important distinction between classes of systems and treat them accordingly.

Shared memory systems

Shared memory systems have multiple CPUs all of which share the same address space. This means that the knowledge of where data is stored is of no concern to the user as there is only one memory accessed by all CPUs on an equal basis. Shared memory systems can be both SIMD and MIMD. Single-CPU vector processors can be regarded as an example of the former, while the multi-CPU models of these machines are examples of the latter. We will sometimes use the abbreviations SM-SIMD and SM-MIMD for the two subclasses.

Distributed memory systems

In this case each CPU has its own associated memory. The CPUs are connected by some network and may exchange data between their respective memories when required. In contrast to shared memory machines the user must be aware of the location of the data in the local memories and will have to move or distribute these data explicitly when needed. Again, distributed memory systems may be either SIMD or MIMD. The first class of SIMD systems mentioned which operate in lock step, all have distributed memories associated to the processors. As we will see, distributed-memory MIMD systems exhibit a large variety in the topology of their connecting network. The details of this topology are largely hidden from the user, which is quite helpful with respect to portability of applications. For the distributed-memory systems we will sometimes use DM-SIMD and DM-MIMD to indicate the two subclasses. Although the difference between shared- and distributed memory machines seems clear cut, this is not always entirely the case from user's point of view. For instance, the late Kendall Square Research systems employed the idea of "virtual shared memory" on a hardware level. Virtual shared memory can also be simulated at the programming level: A specification of High Performance FORTRAN (HPF) was published in 1993, which by means of compiler directives distributes the data over the available processors. Therefore, the system on which HPF is implemented in this case will look like a shared memory machine to the user. Other vendors of Massively Parallel Processing systems (sometimes called MPP systems), like HP and SGI/Cray, also are able to support proprietary virtual shared-memory programming models due to the fact that these physically distributed memory systems are able to address the whole collective address space. So, for the user such systems have one global address space spanning all of the memory in the system. We will say a little more about the structure of such systems in the ccNUMA section. In addition, packages like TreadMarks provide a virtual shared memory environment for networks of workstations.

6.6 Distributed Processing Systems

Another trend that has come up in the last few years is distributed processing. This takes the DM-MIMD concept one step further: instead of many integrated processors in one or several boxes, workstations, mainframes, etc., are connected by (Gigabit) Ethernet, FDDI, or otherwise and set to work concurrently on tasks in the same program. Conceptually, this is not different from DM-MIMD computing, but the communication between processors is often orders of magnitude slower. Many packages to realise distributed computing are available. Examples of these are PVM (standing for Parallel Virtual Machine), and MPI (Message Passing Interface). This style of programming, called the "message passing" model has becomes so much accepted that PVM and MPI have been adopted by virtually all major vendors of distributed-memory MIMD systems and even on shared-memory MIMD systems for compatibility reasons. In addition there is a tendency to cluster shared-memory systems, for instance by HiPPI channels, to obtain systems with a very high computational power. E.g., the NEC SX-5, and the SGI/Cray SV1 have this structure. So, within the clustered nodes a shared-memory programming style can be used while between clusters message passing should be used.

6.7 ccNUMA machines

As already mentioned in the introduction, a trend can be observed to build systems that have a rather small (up to 16) number of RISC processors that are tightly integrated in a cluster, a Symmetric Multi-Processing (SMP) node. A 1-stage crossbar virtually always connects the processors in such a node while a less costly network connects these clusters.

This is similar to the policy mentioned for large vector processor ensembles mentioned above but with the important difference that all of the processors can access all of the address space. Therefore, such systems can be considered as SM-MIMD machines. On the other hand, because the memory is physically distributed, it cannot be guaranteed that a data access operation always will be satisfied within the same time. Therefore such machines are called ccNUMA systems where ccNUMA stands for Cache Coherent Non-Uniform Memory Access. The term "Cache Coherent" refers to the fact that for all CPUs any variable that is to be used must have a consistent value. Therefore, is must be assured that the caches that provide these variables are also consistent in this respect. There are various ways to ensure that the caches of the CPUs are coherent. One is the snoopy bus protocol in which the caches listen in on transport of variables to any of the CPUs and update their own copies of these variables if they have them. Another way is the directory memory, a special part of memory, which enables to keep track of the all copies of variables and of their validity.

For all practical purposes we can classify these systems as being SM-MIMD machines also because special assisting hardware/software (such as a directory memory) has been incorporated to establish a single system image although the memory is physically distributed.

7. Linux Super Computers

Supercomputers traditionally have been expensive, highly customized designs purchased by a select group of customers, but the industry is being overhauled by comparatively mainstream technologies such as Intel processors, InfiniBand high-speed connections (see also Myricom, and Fibre Channel storage networks that have become fast enough to accomplish many tasks.

The new breed of supercomputers usually involves numerous two-processor servers bolted into racks and joined with special high-speed networks into a cluster.

201

Linux Networx customers include Los Alamos and Lawrence Livermore national laboratories for nuclear weapons research, Boeing for aeronautic engineering, and Sequenom for genetics research.

About Clusterworx : Clusterworx is the most complete administration tool for monitoring and management of Linux-based cluster systems. Clusterworx increases system uptime, improves cluster efficiency, tracks cluster performance, and removes the hassle from cluster installation and configuration. The primary features of Clusterworx include monitoring of system properties, integrated disk cloning using multicast technology, and event management of node properties through a remotely accessible, easy-to-use graphical user interface (GUI). Some of the system properties monitored include CPU Usage, Memory Usage, Disk I/O, Network Bandwidth, and many more. Additional custom properties can easily be monitored through the use of user-specific plug-ins. Events automate system administration tasks by setting thresholds on these properties and then taking default or custom actions when these values are exceeded.

About Myricom: Myrinet clusters are used for computationally demanding scientific and engineering applications, and for data-intensive web and database applications. All of the major OEM computer companies today offer cluster products. In addition to direct sales, Myricom supplies Myrinet products and software to IBM, HP, Compaq, Sun, NEC, SGI, Cray, and many other OEM and system-integration companies. There are thousands of Myrinet clusters in use worldwide, including several systems with more than 1000 processors.

7.1 Little Linux SuperComputer In Your Garage

Imagine your garage filled with dozens of computers all linked together in a super-powerful Linux cluster. You still have to supply your own hardware, but the geek equivalent of a Mustang GT will become easier to set up and maintain, thanks to new software to be demonstrated at LinuxWorld next week.

The Open Source Cluster Applications Resources (OSCAR) software, being developed by the Open Cluster Group, will allow a non-expert Linux user to set up a cluster in a matter of hours, instead of the days of work it now can take an experienced network administrator to piece one together. Developers of OSCAR are saying it'll be as easy as installing most software. Call it a "supercomputer on a CD."

"We've actually taken it to the point where a typical high school kid who has a little bit of experience with Linux and can get their hands on a couple of extra boxes could set up a cluster at home," says Stephen L. Scott, project leader at the Oak Ridge National Laboratory, one of several organizations working on OSCAR. "You can have a little supercomputer in your garage."

Supercomputing in Linux:

From A step-by-step guide on how to set up a cluster of PCQLinux machines for supercomputing

Shekhar Govindarajan, Friday, May 10, 2002

To keep it simple, we start with a cluster of three machines. One will be the server and the other two will be the nodes. However, plugging in additional nodes is easy and we will tell you the modification to accommodate additional nodes. Instead of two nodes, you can have a single node. So, even if you have two PCs, you can build a cluster. We suggest that you go through the article Understanding Clustering, page 42, which explains what a cluster is and what server and nodes mean in a cluster before you get started.

*Set up server hardware *you should have at least a 2 GB or bigger hard disk on the server. It should have a graphics card that is supported by PCQLinux 7.1 and a floppy drive. You also need to plug in two network cards preferably the faster PCI cards instead of ISA supported by PCQLinux.

Why two network cards? Adhering to the standards for cluster set-ups, if the server node needs to be connected to the outside (external) network? Internet or your private network? the nodes in the cluster must be on a separate network. This is needed if you want to remotely execute programs on the server. If not, you can do away with a second network card for the external network. For example, at PCQ Labs, we have our regular machines plugged in the 192.168.1.0 network. We selected the network 172.16.0.0 for the cluster nodes. Hence, on the server, one network card (called external interface) will be connected to the Labs network and the other network card (internal interface) will be connected to a switch. We used a 100/10 Mbps switch. A 100 Mbps switch is recommended because the faster the speed of the network, the faster is the message passing. All cluster nodes will also be connected to this switch.

*PCQLinux on server *If you already have a machine with PCQLinux 7.1, including the X Window (KDE or GNOME), installed you can use it as a server machine. In this case you may skip the following steps for installation. If this machine has a firewall (ipchains or iptables) setup, remove all strict restrictive rules, as it will hinder communication between the server and the nodes. The 'medium' level of firewall rules in PCQLinux is suitable. After the cluster set up, you may selectively enable the rules, if required.

If you haven't installed PCQLinux on the machine, opt for custom system install and manual partitioning. Create the swap and / (ROOT) partitions. If you are shown the 1024 cylinder limit problem, you may also have to create a /boot partition of about 50 MB. In the network configuration, fill in the hostname (say, server. cluster.net), IP address of the gateway/router on your network, and the IP of a DNS server (if any) running on your network. Leave other field to their defaults. We will set up the IP addresses for network cards after the installation. Select 'Medium' for the firewall configuration. We now come to the package-selection wizard. You don't need to install all the packages. Besides the packages selected by default, select 'Development' and 'Kernel Development' packages. These provide various libraries and header files for writing programs and are useful if you will develop applications on the cluster. You will need the X Window system because we will use a graphical tool for cluster set up and configuration. By default, GNOME is selected as the Window Manager. If you are comfortable using KDE, select it instead. By suggesting that you select only a few packages for install, we aim at a minimal installation. However, if you wish to install other packages like your favorite text editor, network management utilities or a Web server, then you can select them. Make sure that you set up your graphics card and monitor correctly.

After the installation finishes, reboot into PCQLinux. Log in as root.

*Set up OSCAR *Mount this month's CD and copy the file oscar-1.2.1.tar.gz from the directory system/cdrom/ unltdlinux/linux on the CD to /root. Uncompress and extract the archive as:

tar -zxvf oscar-1.2.1.tar.gz

This will extract the files in a directory named oscar-1.2.1 within /root directory.

OSCAR installs Linux on the nodes from the server across the network. For this, it constructs an image file from RPM packages. This image file is in turn picked up by the nodes to install PCQLinux onto them. The OSCAR version we've given on the CD is customized for RedHat 7.1. Though PCQLinux 7.1 is also based on RedHat 7.1, some RPMs with PCQLinux are of more recent versions than the ones required by OSCAR. OSCAR constructs the image out of a list of RPMs specified in sample.rpmlist in the subdirectory oscarsamples in oscar-1.2.1. You have to replace this file with the one customized for PCQLinux RPMs. We have given a file named sample.rpmlist on this month's CD in the directory system/cdrom/unltdlinux /linux. Overwrite the file sample.rpmlist in the oscarsamples directory with this file.

---

*Copy PCQLinux RPMs to /tftpboot/rpm
*For creating the image, OSCAR will look for the PCQLinux RPMs in the directory /tftpboot/rpm. Create a directory /tftpboot and a subdirectory named rpm within it

mkdir /tftpboot
mkdir /tftpboot/rpm

Next, copy all the PCQLinux RPMs from both the CDs to /tftpboot/rpm directory. Insert CD 1 (PCQLinux CD 1, given with our July 2001 issue) and issue the following commands:

mount /mnt/cdrom
cd /mnt/cdrom/RedHat/RPMS
cp *.rpm /tftpboot/ rpm
cd
umount /mnt/cdrom

Insert CD 2 (given with the July 2001 issue) and issue the above commands again.

Note. If you are tight at the disk space, you don't need to copy all the RPMs to /tftpboot/rpm. You can copy only the RPMs listed in sample.rpmlist file. Copy only the required RPMs.

*Copy required RPMs
*Type the following in a Linux text editor and save the file as copyrpms.sh

#!/bin/bash
rpms_path="/mnt/cdrom/RedHat/RPMS/"

```
rpms_list="/root/oscar-1.2.1/oscarsamples/sample.rpmlist"
mount /mnt/cdrom
while read line
do file="$rpms_path$line.i386.rpm"
if [ -f $file ]
then
cp $file /tftpboot/rpm
else file="$rpms_path$line.noarch.rpm"
if [ -f $file ]
then
cp $file /tftpboot/rpm
else file="$rpms_path$line.i586.rpm"
if [ -f $file ]
then
cp $file /tftpboot/rpm
else file="$rpms_path$line.i686.rpm"
if [ -f $file ]
then
cp $file /tftpboot/rpm
fi
fi
fi
fi
done < $rpms_list
eject
```

Give executable permissions to the file as:

```
chmod +x copyrpms.sh
```

Assuming that you have created the directory /tftpboot/rpm, insert
PCQLinux CD 1 (don't mount it) and issue:
./copyrpms

When all the RPMs from the CD are copied, the CD drive will eject. Next,
insert CD 2 and issue ./copyrpms again.

*Fix glitch in PCQLinux
*On this month's CD we have carried the zlib
rpm 'zlib-1.1.3-22.i386.rpm' which you can find in the directory
system/cdrom/ unltdlinux/linux on the CD. (We had given this on our July
CD as well, but the file was corrupt.) Install the RPM as:

```
rpm -ivh zlib-1.1.3-22.i386.rpm
```

Copy this file to /tftpboot/rpm directory. This will prompt you to
overwrite the corrupted zlib RPM, already in the directory. Go for it.

*Set up networking
*Linux names network cards or interfaces as eth0, eth1, eth2. In our
case eth0 is the internal interface and eth1 is the external interface.
We assign eth0, an IP address of 172.16.0.1. Since we are running a DHCP
server on the PCQ Labs network, we will set eth1 to obtain IP address

from the DHCP server. If you are using a single network card for the cluster network, skip setting up the second card.

Launch X Window. Launch a terminal window within GNOME or KDE and issue the command netcfg. This will pop up a graphical network configurator. Click on the Interfaces tab. To set up the internal interface, click on eth0 and then on edit. For IP address, enter 172.16.0.1 and for the netmask enter 255.255.255.0. Click on 'Activate interface at boot time'. For 'Interface configuration protocol' select 'none' from the drop-down list.

To set up the external interface, select eth1 and click on edit. If you are running a DHCP server, select dhcp from the drop down list. Else, enter a free IP address (say, 192.168.1.23), the associated netmask (say, 255.255.255.0) and select none from the drop-down list. In either case, make sure to click on 'Activate interface at boot time'.

Highlight eth0 and click on the button 'Activate'. Do the same for eth1. Finally, click on save and quit the configurator.

Issue the command, ifconfig to check whether the network interfaces are up and have been given the correct IP addresses.
You are now ready to start Oscar.

*Run OSCAR
*In the terminal window, change to oscar-1.2.2 directory and issue the command:

./install_cluster eth0

Replace eth0 with the name of the internal interface in your case. You will see text flowing in the window. After a couple of minutes, the graphical wizard of OSCAR will pop up. OSCAR installation calls cluster nodes as clients

*Build image from RPMs
*Click on 'Build Oscar Client Image'. We assume that all the node machines will have IDE hard disks. If you are using SCSI hard disk in the nodes, you need to change the Disk Partition File. Refer to the OSCAR installation documentation on the CD. When finished, a message 'Successfully created image oscarimage' will pop up.

*Tell OSCAR about the nodes
*Click on the button 'Define OSCAR clients'. Here you should see the domain name, starting IP and subnet mast, pre-filled with cluster.net, 172.16.0.2 and 255.255. 255.0. With 'Number of hosts' you specify the number of nodes. As per the OSCAR documentation, OSCAR supports up to 100 nodes or may be more. But it hasn't been experimented with arbitrary large number of nodes. In our case we fill in two. If you are experimenting with two machines, one server and the other the node, then fill in one.

In OSCAR once you define the number of nodes you cannot change it after the cluster is installed. You need to again start from the beginning, i.e., from the step when we issued 'install_cluster'

Note. If for any reason you need to start again, before issuing ./install_cluster, execute the script named start_over located in the subdirectory scripts as:

/root/oscar-1.2.1/script/start_over'

Clicking on the 'Add clients' button will show 'Successfully created clients' after a couple of seconds.

*Set up the nodes *
Before carrying out the subsequent steps in OSCAR installation, connect the network cards of the node machines to the switch and set them up to boot from floppy from their BIOS.

*Set up nodes to network
*We come back to OSCAR installation wizard running on the server machine. Click on the button 'Set up Networking'. In the right frame you will see a tree-like structure as shown in the screenshot. In our case, the two nodes are given a hostname of oscarnode1.cluster.net and oscarnode2. cluster.net. They are assigned IP addresses 172.16.0.2 and 172.16. 0.3 respectively. Next, we assign the MAC (Media Access Control) address of the nodes to the listed IP addresses. This can be done by booting the nodes using a floppy created by OSCAR or by networking booting them. For the latter refer to the OSCAR documentation given on the CD.

Click on the button 'Build AutoInstall Floppy'. This will pop up a terminal window. Insert a blank floppy in the server and click 'y' to continue. After the terminal window disappears, click on the button 'Collect MAC addresses' in the OSCAR window. Insert the floppy in one of the node machines and power it on. The machine will boot from the floppy. Press enter at the boot: prompt. After some time, the MAC address of the node will show up in the left frame. Suppose we want to assign the IP address 172.16.0.1 to this node. Click on the MAC address in the left and on the 'osacrnde1.cluster.net' in the right frame. Then, click on 'Assign MAC to node'.

*Assign IP addresses to the nodes of the cluster
*Switch off the node machine. Now boot the second node machine from the same floppy. As before, the MAC address of the second node will appear in the left frame. Assign it to oscarnode2. cluster.net.

If you want to plug in more node machines, repeat the above process for them. When done, click on the button 'Stop collecting' on the OSCAR window.

After shutting down all the node machines, click on the button 'Configure DHCP Server'. Then click on the close button in the 'MAC address collection' window.

*PCQLinux on the nodes

*Next, boot the first node machine again from the floppy. This time the node machine will install PCQLinux 7.1 from the network. When done, a message, as following, will be shown:

I have done for ' seconds. Reboot me already

Take out the floppy and reboot the node machine. This time it should boot from the hard disk. If everything has gone well, you will boot into PCOLinux 7.1. While booting, PCQLinux will detect and prompt you to set up hardware like mouse, graphics card, sound card etc on the nodes.

*Problem: No active partition
*If you are shown an error during booting which says no active partition, then boot from a Windows bootable floppy or CD. Launch fdisk and select option2 (Set active partition). Set partition 1 of type non-dos and about 31 MB in size as active. This is the /boot partition from where the kernel boot image resides.

*Test networking of nodes
*On the server, open another terminal window and issue:

/root/oscar-1.2.2/scripts/ping_clients

If there is no problem with the networking, you will be shown 'All clients responded'. Else check whether all nodes are powered on, defects in network cables, hub/ switch ports etc. From now on, ideally, you don't need to work physically on the node machines. Hence you can plug off the monitor, keyboard, mouse, etc from the node machines. If the node machines need to be accessed and worked upon, you should use SSH (Secure Shell), similar to telnet but secure, to access them from the server.

*All done
*Click on 'Complete Cluster Setup' and then on 'Test cluster Setup'. This will pop up a terminal window and prompt you to enter a non-root username. Enter 'shekhar' (say). If the user account does not exist on the server machine, it will be created. In the latter case, you will be prompted for a password for the new account. Click on the 'Quit' button on the OSCAR window. Reboot the server machine.

*Test the cluster
*To test the cluster, log in as the user that you created above (shekhar in our case) and issue:

cd OSCAR_test
./text_cluster

Enter the number of nodes when prompted (two in our case). For the number of processors on each client enters 1 (assuming uniprocessor machines). The test verifies the running of PBS and runs example programs coded using LAM, MPICH, and PVM libraries by dispatching them through PBS to the nodes. You can see pbs_mom (see Understanding Clustering, page 42) running on the nodes by issuing the command 'ps 'e

| grep pbs_mom' on the nodes.

If there are no error messages in the output, congratulations, you have your supercomputer up and running. Our cluster setup qualifies to be called a Beowulf cluster because it has been built using easily available hardware, free and open-source software, the /home directory on the server is exported to all the nodes via NFS (you can check this by issuing the command 'mount' on the nodes), and finally the server and nodes can execute command and scripts remotely on each other via SSH. Using the libraries installed on the cluster, you can start developing or executing cluster-aware applications on the server. The compilers for them (like, gcc, g++) are same as with PCQLinux.

Shekhar Govindarajan

---

8. Neural Network Processors

NNs are models of biological neural networks and some are not, but historically, much of the inspiration for the field of NNs came from the desire to produce artificial systems capable of sophisticated, perhaps "intelligent", computations similar to those that the human brain routinely performs, and thereby possibly to enhance our understanding of the human brain.

Most NNs have some sort of "training" rule whereby the weights of connections are adjusted on the basis of data. In other words, NNs "learn" from examples (as children learn to recognize dogs from examples of dogs) and exhibit some capability for generalization beyond the training data.

NNs normally have great potential for parallelism, since the computations of the components are largely independent of each other. Some people regard massive parallelism and high connectivity to be defining characteristics of NNs, but such requirements rule out various simple models, such as simple linear regression (a minimal feedforward net with only two units plus bias), which are usefully regarded as special cases of NNs.

Some definitions of Neural Network (NN) are as follows:

- According to the DARPA Neural Network Study : A neural network is a system composed of many simple processing elements operating in parallel whose function is determined by network structure, connection strengths, and the processing performed at computing elements or nodes.
- According to Haykin: A neural network is a massively parallel-distributed processor that has a natural propensity for storing experiential knowledge and making it available for use. It resembles the brain in two respects:
    - The network through a learning process acquires knowledge.
    - Interneuron connection strengths known as synaptic weights are used to store the knowledge.
- According to Nigrin: A neural network is a circuit composed of a very large number of simple processing elements that are neurally based. Each element

operates only on local information. Furthermore each element operates asynchronously; thus there is no overall system clock.

- According to Zurada: Artificial neural systems, or neural networks, are physical cellular systems, which can acquire, store, and utilize experiential knowledge.

Visit the following sites for more info on Neural Network Processors

- Omers Neural Network pointers
  http://www.cs.cf.ac.uk/User/O.F.Rana/neural.html
- FAQ site ftp://ftp.sas.com/pub/neural/FAQ.html
- Automation corp Neural Network Processor hardware

---

9. Related URLs

Visit following locators, which are related -

- Color Vim editor http://metalab.unc.edu/LDP/HOWTO/Vim-HOWTO.html
- Source code control system http://metalab.unc.edu/LDP/HOWTO/CVS-HOWTO.html
- Linux goodies main site http://www.milkywaygalaxy.freeservers.com and mirrors at http://aldev0.webjump.com, angelfire, geocities, virtualave, 50megs, theglobe, NBCi, Terrashare, Fortunecity, Freewebsites, Tripod, Spree, Escalix, Httpcity, Freeservers.

---

10. Other Formats of this Document

This document is published in 14 different formats namely - DVI, Postscript, Latex, Adobe Acrobat PDF, LyX, GNU-info, HTML, RTF(Rich Text Format), Plain-text, Unix man pages, single HTML file, SGML (Linuxdoc format), SGML (Docbook format), MS WinHelp format.

This howto document is located at -

- http://www.linuxdoc.org and click on HOWTOs and search for howto document name using CTRL+f or ALT+f within the web-browser.

You can also find this document at the following mirrors sites -

- http://www.caldera.com/LDP/HOWTO
- http://www.linux.ucla.edu/LDP
- http://www.cc.gatech.edu/linux/LDP
- http://www.redhat.com/mirrors/LDP
- Other mirror sites near you (network-address-wise) can be found at http://www.linuxdoc.org/mirrors.html select a site and go to directory /LDP/HOWTO/xxxxx-HOWTO.html

- You can get this HOWTO document as a single file tar ball in HTML, DVI, Postscript or SGML formats from -
ftp://www.linuxdoc.org/pub/Linux/docs/HOWTO/other-formats/ and
http://www.linuxdoc.org/docs.html#howto
- Plain text format is in: ftp://www.linuxdoc.org/pub/Linux/docs/HOWTO and
http://www.linuxdoc.org/docs.html#howto
- Single HTML file format is in: http://www.linuxdoc.org/docs.html#howto

  Single HTML file can be created with command (see man sgml2html) -
  sgml2html -split 0 xxxxhowto.sgml

- Translations to other languages like French, German, Spanish, Chinese, Japanese are in ftp://www.linuxdoc.org/pub/Linux/docs/HOWTO and http://www.linuxdoc.org/docs.html#howto any help from you to translate to other languages is welcome.

The document is written using a tool called "SGML-Tools" which can be got from -
http://www.sgmltools.org compiling the source you will get the following commands like

- sgml2html xxxxhowto.sgml (to generate html file)
- sgml2html -split 0 xxxxhowto.sgml (to generate a single page html file)
- sgml2rtf xxxxhowto.sgml (to generate RTF file)
- sgml2latex xxxxhowto.sgml (to generate latex file)

10.1 Acrobat PDF format

PDF file can be generated from postscript file using either acrobat **distill** or **Ghostscript**. And postscript file is generated from DVI, which in turn is generated from LaTex file. You can download distill software from http://www.adobe.com. Given below is a sample session:

```
bash$ man sgml2latex
bash$ sgml2latex filename.sgml
bash$ man dvips
bash$ dvips -o filename.ps filename.dvi
bash$ distill filename.ps
bash$ man ghostscript
bash$ man ps2pdf
bash$ ps2pdf input.ps output.pdf
bash$ acroread output.pdf &
```

Or you can use Ghostscript command **ps2pdf**. ps2pdf is a work-alike for nearly all the functionality of Adobe's Acrobat Distiller product: it converts PostScript files to Portable Document Format (PDF) files. **ps2pdf** is implemented as a very small command script (batch file) that invokes Ghostscript, selecting a special "output device" called **pdfwrite**. In order to use ps2pdf, the pdfwrite device must be included in the makefile when Ghostscript was compiled; see the documentation on building Ghostscript for details.

211

10.2 Convert Linuxdoc to Docbook format

This document is written in linuxdoc SGML format. The Docbook SGML format supercedes the linuxdoc format and has lot more features than linuxdoc. The linuxdoc is very simple and is easy to use. To convert linuxdoc SGML file to Docbook SGML use the program **ld2db.sh** and some perl scripts. The ld2db output is not 100% clean and you need to use the **clean_ld2db.pl** perl script. You may need to manually correct few lines in the document.

- Download ld2db program from http://www.dcs.gla.ac.uk/~rrt/docbook.html or from Milkyway Galaxy site
- Download the cleanup_ld2db.pl perl script from from Milkyway Galaxy site

The ld2db.sh is not 100% clean, you will get lots of errors when you run

```
bash$ ld2db.sh file-linuxdoc.sgml db.sgml
bash$ cleanup.pl db.sgml > db_clean.sgml
bash$ gvim db_clean.sgml
bash$ docbook2html db.sgml
```

And you may have to manually edit some of the minor errors after running the perl script. For e.g. you may need to put closing tag < /Para> for each < Listitem>

10.3 Convert to MS WinHelp format

You can convert the SGML howto document to Microsoft Windows Help file, first convert the sgml to html using:

```
bash$ sgml2html xxxxhowto.sgml      (to generate html file)
bash$ sgml2html -split 0   xxxxhowto.sgml (to generate a single page html file)
```

Then use the tool HtmlToHlp. You can also use sgml2rtf and then use the RTF files for generating winhelp files.

10.4 Reading various formats

In order to view the document in dvi format, use the xdvi program. The xdvi program is located in tetex-xdvi*.rpm package in Redhat Linux which can be located through ControlPanel | Applications | Publishing | TeX menu buttons. To read dvi document give the command -

```
xdvi -geometry 80x90 howto.dvi
man xdvi
```

And resize the window with mouse. To navigate use Arrow keys, Page Up, Page Down keys, also you can use 'f', 'd', 'u', 'c', 'l', 'r', 'p', 'n' letter keys to move up, down, center, next page, previous page etc. To turn off expert menu press 'x'.

You can read postscript file using the program 'gv' (ghostview) or 'ghostscript'. The ghostscript program is in ghostscript*.rpm package and gv program is in gv*.rpm package in Redhat Linux which can be located through ControlPanel | Applications | Graphics menu buttons. The gv program is much more user friendly than ghostscript.

Also ghostscript and gv are available on other platforms like OS/2, Windows 95 and NT, you view this document even on those platforms.

- Get ghostscript for Windows 95, OS/2, and for all OSes from
  http://www.cs.wisc.edu/~ghost

To read postscript document give the command -

```
gv howto.ps
ghostscript howto.ps
```

You can read HTML format document using Netscape Navigator, Microsoft Internet explorer, Redhat Baron Web browser or any of the 10 other web browsers.

You can read the latex, LyX output using LyX a X-Windows front end to latex.

---

11. Copyright

Copyright policy is GNU/GPL as per LDP (Linux Documentation project). LDP is a GNU/GPL project. Additional restrictions are - you must retain the author's name, email address and this copyright notice on all the copies. If you make any changes or additions to this document then you should intimate all the authors of this document.

Index

T

U

V

W

Z